PROVING RICHARD CRANCH

A Report of Investigation On Furniture, Family, and a Unique American Story

CARLEEN A. WATTS

NANTY'S HOUSE

PUBLISHING

Phoenix, Arizona

Nanty's House

Publishing

Phoenix, Arizona

This edition April 2022
Copyright © 2022 by Carleen Watts

Profile of Richard Cranch used with kind permission from the Massachusetts Historical Society.

Nanty's House Publishing is an assumed business name of Watts Consulting Services, LLC.

For some full-color images of George's secretary and more items from the Dawes Collection, visit WattsConsultingServices.com. For speaking engagements or information about bulk purchases, please contact Carleen Watts at cawatts99@outlook.com.

Cover Design & Image: Wanna Johansson
Editorial and Interior Design: Jenefer Angell, Passionfruit Projects

Manufactured in the United States of America
ISBN: 979-8-9852259-0-7 (paper)

To the memory of my mother, Gloria Ann Watts,
caretaker of George's secretary

CONTENTS

Introduction: The Allegations 7

1. The Chain of Custody..13

2. The Inquiry..23

3. The Hiatus 39

4. The Investigation...51

5. The Evidence, Part I: The Dawes Collection 71

6. The Intent 95

7. The Evidence, Part II: Nanty's Letters 117

8. The Closing Argument..141

9. The Conclusion...147

Appendix A: The Dawes Family Tree.....................................151

Appendix B: The Cranch Family Tree.....................................152

Appendix C: Daweses Marry Greenleafs 153

Appendix D: The Journey of George's Secretary 154

Acknowledgments 155

About the Author...159

George's secretary

INTRODUCTION
The Allegations

When I inherited an old eighteenth-century carved mahogany secretary — a writing desk with a bookcase attached — given to my mother in 1955 from an old gentleman named George Minot Dawes, it came with two unsubstantiated allegations: it was a Dawes family heirloom and it had been crafted in Boston sometime before or during the Revolutionary War. I had grown up seeing this grand old piece of carved wood every day in my home and while I had no reason to doubt the allegations, by nature and training I'm not one to leave unsubstantiated claims unaddressed. So I did the only thing I know how: I opened an investigation to learn the secretary's true identity and restore its heritage.

Was I qualified to take on such a daunting task? Having spent thirty-two years of my life as a Special Agent investigating financial fraud against the United States government, I believed I was. I served as a Special Agent for the US Departments of Agriculture, Defense, Veterans Affairs, and the Postal Service, working within each department's Office of Inspector General (OIG), and as Senior Instructor at the Federal Law Enforcement Training Center in Glynco, Georgia, teaching fellow Special Agents how to investigate financial fraud. I became a Certified Fraud Examiner in 1996. A few years after retiring, I returned temporarily to fight fraud for the Special Inspector General for Afghanistan Reconstruction (SIGAR) in both Kabul, Afghanistan, and Arlington, Virginia.

Special Agents working within the OIG community focus primarily on allegations of fraud, waste, and mismanagement occurring inside a government agency. When a news broadcaster uses the term "government watchdog," they are usually referring to the agency's OIG.

Just like their Special Agent counterparts who work for those more well-known three-letter federal law enforcement agencies such as the FBI, IRS, and DEA, OIG Special Agents carry guns, make arrests, execute search warrants, serve subpoenas, interview subjects and witnesses, and present their case findings to an Assistant United States Attorney for prosecution. Violators who are successful defrauding one government agency often cannot resist the temptation to unleash their newfound skills upon others, resulting in a multiagency investigation with agents from each OIG working together as a team.

Fraud is all about greed and the clever schemes people invent to obtain what is not legally theirs, whether that be money or other valuable assets. Special Agents who investigate fraud possess a specific skill set: they are detail-oriented individuals who can effectively manage enormous amounts of information generated from countless bank accounts, public and private records, and interviews. They are able to identify key associations between identified targets, their businesses, and their financial transactions. They connect these same targets to relevant and specific events or activities that enabled the fraud to occur. They have the patience and perseverance to see their case through after months or even years of investigative activity. Above all, fraud investigators, like any other law enforcement officer, are able to remain impartial and objective throughout the entire process. Their job is to gather the evidence and put the pieces together to tell a story—a truthful, fact-supported story, nothing more.

Detective Joe Friday said it best in the old series *Dragnet*, "Just the facts ma'am."

In other words, I was in fact just the person to investigate the origins of this grand piece of furniture that now sat in my home. Since I was well-equipped with these skills and experience, I was convinced my new tenant's life story would require a few easy hours of research.

I could not have been more wrong.

In the end it took all my specialized skills to find and unlock forgotten treasure chests containing the evidence necessary to resurrect a 250-year-old story and timeline. And this complex and challenging investigation transformed itself into a parasite, affixing itself to my life on and off again for over twenty years, always in my thoughts. This was by far the coldest case I had ever worked, full of unexpected detours that triggered more aggravating moments than I encountered in my entire professional career. At the same time, no other case produced the degree of satisfaction I felt than from this one once the investigative leads were completed and the truth was finally known. My long-term efforts secured this special piece of furniture with its original identity, a documented history, and (to my delight) more value.

Why Take on This Almost Impossible Task?

As a child, my mother dragged me into countless antique shops whenever she took notice of a new opening in an area of town reserved for ancient artifacts. Inside these dark, musty chambers, I loved exploring all of the odd-looking items lining the walls: desks, dining-room tables, chairs, bookcases, bedframes, and side tables. I particularly liked items once owned by historic people, and the things whose purpose or use posed a mystery to me.

Perhaps my investigative curiosity was already beginning to surface at this young age. Unlike the stories and photographs in my school history books, I could actually touch the surface of these items and look inside each drawer and hidden compartment in search of clues to explain its true function. Discovering how these items had been used in earlier days gave me insight into the daily lives and hardships of my grandparents and great-grandparents. I quickly learned to appreciate how easy my life was compared to previous generations.

Unfortunately for my mother, my family's financial status did not allow her to purchase many of the unique pieces she found and admired. However, her thirst for acquiring antiques would be quenched when she met George Minot Dawes (1884–1972), a direct descendant of Revolutionary War patriot Colonel Thomas Dawes.

Before he died, George gave my mother his family's secretary, hereafter referred to as "George's secretary." Regrettably, George never mentioned specifically who in his historic family had once owned this beautiful monstrosity. When pushed for details, he would simply say, "It's a family piece." George's secretary, along with its uncertain and mysterious chain of custody, became part of my own household when my mother decided it was time to downsize.

A Report of Investigation

As mentioned, the Special Agent in me was naturally attracted to the mystery of its origin and ownership and I felt compelled to pursue it. What you are about to read is my "report of investigation" for this case. Special Agents write these types of reports to identify the subject or target of the investigation, the alleged criminal or civil statutes violated, and to summarize all the documented evidence collected to prove or disprove the alleged violations. It is an extremely straightforward report that must not contain or express any of the Special Agent's private or professional opinions, theories, or conclusions.

As the lead and sole investigator for this case, I admit to breaking most of the basic rules Special Agents are trained to follow. This case became personal — extremely personal. Which means you will be hearing my opinions, theories, and conclusions as I explain each investigative step and technique used to solve this lingering mystery. I also included all of what I like to call my OSOD (Oh shit, oh dear!) discoveries. These are the rare moments when agents finally come across that hard-to-find, case-proving evidence. We all react a little differently to these discoveries but you often see agents running around their office announcing their findings to anyone willing to listen. You might even see them doing a happy dance in a nearby conference room.

Fraud investigators wait patiently for these moments, like treasure hunters looking for buried gold and silver on a deserted island. Except their treasure is hidden evidence buried somewhere within the mounds of paper and electronic data they routinely seize and review. One small OSOD discovery can provide the motivation agents frequently need to persevere in this butt-numbing environment they try their best to maneuver through. If this newly found treasure (evidence) is proven to be reliable, it may connect the target of the investigation directly to the alleged violation, pushing the case that much closer to the finish line, a line that often results in an arrest and indictment.

For obvious reasons, my OSOD outbursts and other case-stimulating moments are never included in an official report of investigation. Here, however, I take the liberty of giving you all a behind-the-scenes look at what goes on in the mind and soul of a Special Agent during an investigation. Strangely, this case, like no other, pushed the boundaries a step further into the realm of what I call the "bizarre and unbelievable" — incidents I never saw coming or could have imagined, each leaving me with a spine-tingling chill at the time of its discovery.

As I lay out my investigative steps and the evidence I uncovered along the way, please keep in mind that I am only a Special Agent. My sole job was to identify and legally obtain evidence. With that came the chore of identifying witnesses who could testify in court as to the authenticity of each piece of evidence I collected. I am not a professional historic researcher or scholar. Quite frankly, I am in awe of such individuals and marvel at the thoroughness of their documentation processes and ability to seek out historic truths and relics. Their investigative skills put most Special Agents to shame.

So, if you are looking for detailed footnotes on each of the items presented in this report of investigation, you will not find them. What you will find is an entirely truthful and sometimes mind-boggling account of my amazing journey back in time as I searched for evidence to identify and prove who once owned George's secretary. Get ready to meet real-life souls who lived in the eighteenth and nineteenth centuries, souls that continue to haunt and entertain me to this day.

While there is no federal or state statute against owning an eighteenth-century secretary, I took the allegations as seriously as (if not more than) any case before it with the one and only goal to identify and prove who in George's family had previously owned his magnificent secretary. Applying criminal investigative techniques was a successful means to this end.

1

The Chain of Custody

In 1995 I became the owner and caretaker of George's secretary. This monstrosity had sat in my parent's home for over forty years under the loving protection of my mother, Ann Watts. As often happens in one's later years, and after losing a spouse, she decided to downsize, and needed to pass on the care and maintenance of this aging piece of wood to the next generation. (Me.)

My mother in her turn had received the piece from George Minot Dawes in 1955, along with some other Dawes family collectibles (a.k.a. "The Dawes Collection"). Being the extremely private man he was, George offered scant information about this "family piece," and never spoke openly about his family ancestry either. If he had, it would have been a fascinating lesson in early American history.

The Dawes genealogy begins with William Dawes of Sudbury, born in 1620 in Suffolk County, England. Within the Dawes Collection was an original 1878 edition of Henry Holland's book *William Dawes and His Ride with Paul Revere: An Essay Read Before the New England Historic Genealogical Society on June 7, AD 1876; To Which Is Appended a Genealogy of the Dawes Family*. This book was published exclusively for members of the Dawes family, not the public eye. It includes hundreds of Dawes family members born up to the publication date. Printing was limited to one hundred copies. At the time of publication, it was common for a book's owner to inscribe their name inside the front cover. The signature penned inside this edition — Richard Cranch Dawes — indicated the book originally belonged to George's father.

In addition to the Holland book, the Dawes Collection included personal family items such as artwork, a game table, jewelry, photographs, original newspaper clippings, a young girl's stitch sampler (circa 1840), endless pieces of silverware, and the one piece I always admired as a child: George's personalized birthday cup. Made of sterling silver, an ornate decoration covered the cup's lower half. The upper half was smooth and engraved with the inscription, "George Minot Dawes, From His Grandmother, MED." On the bottom, another inscription, "Born Nov 20th 1884."

My Mother: The Novice Investigator

Any additional details about George's family, his secretary, or these other personal items followed George to his grave in November 1972. By this time, George's secretary had sat inconspicuously in the Watts family home for over sixteen years. In all those years, my mother never looked upon it as being truly hers. It was always referred to as "George's secretary" (and will remain so as long as it resides within a Watts home). But with George gone, my mother felt a need to find out more about the permanent boarder who continued to take up space in our living room. She asked herself, "If it were a 'family piece,' who would have been its likely owner?"

The Holland book provided an extensive Dawes family tree following the story of William Dawes's historic yet not-so-well publicized ride alongside Paul Revere. George was born in 1884, six years after the book was published, but his father, Richard

Cranch Dawes, born in Quincy, Massachusetts, in 1838, appeared on page 72.

Colonel Thomas Dawes by Gilbert Stuart, circa 1806

My mother began tracing the male Dawes line backwards from Richard. His father was George Minot Dawes (who "our" George was named after), born in Boston in 1802. Her candidate needed to be much older. Richard's grandfather was another Bostonian named Judge Thomas Dawes. Born in 1757, Thomas would have been in his late teens during the Revolutionary War and was not a suitable candidate either. However, Richard's great-grandfather, Colonel Thomas Dawes, was born in 1731 and played an extensive role during the Revolutionary War. A possible candidate finally emerged from the pack.

My mother knew from conversations with George that he was related to "William Who Rode" but she was never quite sure how. In her research, she learned that the colonel and William shared the same grandfather, another Thomas Dawes (1680–1750), making them cousins. A portrait of Colonel Dawes, painted by artist Gilbert Stuart once hung in the Smithsonian's National Portrait Gallery. I find his resemblance to George quite remarkable.

Now that my mother had identified a possible candidate, how could she determine if the colonel ever owned a secretary? It was 1973, the Internet did not exist yet, which meant conducting historic research the old-fashioned way, by reviewing books and documents from multiple libraries and courthouses. We lived in Sacramento, California, a long way from Boston, so finding relevant publications and documents was difficult and time consuming. Yet to her surprise, after hours of manual searches, she finally came across a book in the California State Library that mentioned a secretary belonging to Colonel Dawes. Yes, the man definitely owned a secretary. But to my mother's disappointment, the piece was accounted for and sitting prominently in a Texas museum. Strike the colonel from the list of possibilities.

My mother had to ask herself: Where to go next? If this beautiful piece did not come down through the colonel's line, what other Dawes lines should she research? Eventually, the many obstacles along the way took the joy out of her research. So she turned her skills inward and used her limited free time to trace her own family roots back to England and Germany.

The mystery surrounding George's secretary would remain unsolved, at least for a few more years.

The Case Is Reassigned

I cannot remember a time when George's secretary was not part of the Watts family home. Our family had become part of its history. But being suddenly handed that responsibility caught me by surprise. Even though I had known I would someday become its custodian, I was not expecting it to happen when it did and the idea was somewhat daunting.

While relocating the piece from my mother's home to mine, I began to understand why my father swore at its monstrous bulk during each of my parents' moves. It was like relocating an aged member of your family to a new home. Fear shoots through your body as movers wrap tape around each fragile hinge and drawer. I held my breath each time one of these muscular men carried the piece in or out of a doorway or up and down a staircase.

Once strategically positioned in my study, I noticed just how impressive the piece looked. How strange it is to grow up with something as grand as this in your childhood home and never actually notice it. There was also something comforting about its presence; a piece of my childhood had become part of my adult home. I sometimes found myself admiring it from the doorway hoping I would hear answers to the questions that bubbled up every time I thought about it. *Who made you? Where else have you lived? What letters were written upon your desktop? What conversations have you overheard? Who in George's family once owned you?*

Think about it; this old piece sat as an observer (a witness) to over 240 years of American history, beginning well before the United States became an independent nation, in the very place where so much of the planning started. Now it was camped out in my home. I swear I could hear it breathe (and sometimes moan from age) each time I stared with admiration. If only I could hear its quiet, humble voice tell me the answers to my questions.

At some point, I knew I would have to take over where my mother left off and find the answers to those lingering allegations. Unfortunately, I (like my mother before me) was caught up with my own career and had little time to dwell on my new tenant's history.

A few days after the move, she came by with more items from the Dawes Collection, ones that were no longer personal favorites: a game table, the Holland book, and three other books, all published before 1880, connected to the history of Braintree and Quincy. There was also a graphite drawing of an old home signed by "C.P.C." dated July 29, 1839. This same house was depicted in another small print my mother had framed. She believed it to be the old Dawes family home in Quincy, Massachusetts. The silver birthday cup would also be staying with me, taking its appropriate place on a shelf inside the bookcase of George's secretary.

Cranch Greenleaf House by C.P. Cranch

About this same time, a new television show was hitting the air waves, *Antiques Roadshow*. People were finding old items in their grandparents' attics that were actually worth hundreds to thousands of dollars. While I did not have a grandparent's attic to rummage through, I did have George's secretary and these other Dawes family pieces. I often wondered what these little treasures might be worth, given their age and "provenance" — what I came to learn was an item's history of ownership. Provenance plays a significant role in determining an antique's value.

In the investigative world, this would be known as the "chain of custody." When evidence is seized during a search or obtained from a witness, in order to introduce the item as evidence at trial, the Special Agent must be able to show who has had custody of the item from the time it was seized until the moment it is presented to a jury. Proof of the item's custody is recorded on a chain of custody form that documents each person who takes possession of the item, the date of and reason for the transfer, and the item's final disposition (returned to the owner, destroyed, and so on).

As I witnessed my mother's painstaking search for information about Colonel Dawes, I knew developing and proving the chain of custody for George's secretary would take time and resources, two things not available to me at that time. With the mahogany monster securely situated in my study, I packed the rest of the Dawes items in a box and placed them in storage waiting for research time to become available. I knew it would not be anytime soon.

By 2000, the Internet provided a new search tool to anyone with a computer and a modem. Various online auction websites began popping up, offering appraisals for all sorts of items. It was a straightforward process. Interested and eager individuals just needed to submit a detailed description of their item along with digital images and, most importantly, a check in exchange for an evaluation by a professional appraiser. It was just like attending the *Antiques Roadshow* but with no travel involved.

I found myself peeking inside the Dawes Collection once again. I wondered if this could be an easy and quick way to find out more about George's secretary and certain other items included in the collection. Mostly, I wanted to know what George's secretary might be worth and if the graphite drawing signed by C.P.C. held any significance or value.

I was also curious about an incredibly old portrait of a young schoolboy painted with oils on a small, 7.5-by-9.5-inch wooden board, a favorite of my mother's that still hung in her home. She had even found an ornate old frame that suited it perfectly. Unfortunately, there were no visible signature markings indicating who might have painted it.

I submitted the required forms for each item, along with my check, to a company called AuctionWatch.com. One week later I received their response and was fascinated by the results. With the obligatory caveat about the limitations of not being able to evaluate the piece in person, the appraiser opined that the painting was American, nineteenth century, with an estimated value of $800 to $1,200. I would need an outside consultant to shed more light on this.

Much to my delight, the appraiser had been able to identify the artist of the graphite drawing as Christopher Pearse Cranch, a well-known artist and transcendentalist of the mid-to-late 1800s. The house, referred to as the Cranch Greenleaf House, belonged to his family in Quincy at one time. The appraiser estimated the value of the drawing to be between $1,200 and

$1,800. They included a short comment about another important Cranch piece:

> In October 1999, a rare japanned American high chest of drawers was sold at Sotheby's in New York. It had descended in the family of the sister of Abigail Adams, Mary Cranch. That high chest was passed down to Margaret Cranch Dawes (of St. Louis) in 1876. It sold for $1.6 million.

Though the Cranch name meant nothing to me, and I failed to see any connection to George's secretary or to his family since the Dawes woman they mentioned was from St. Louis, not Quincy or Boston, I still found this interesting information. I was even more interested in the last appraisal: the appraiser estimated the value of George's secretary between $12,000 and $18,000—based solely upon the description and details I provided. They indicated this value could be greatly affected—as in upwards, to the $30,000 to $40,000 range—if I could demonstrate the item's provenance.

There it was again, like a broken record stuck on a chorus of "Provenance." But this time someone had put a price tag on it. I admit it, those dollar signs were enough to ignite my curiosity but, more seriously, my investigative skills and abilities. One of George's great-great-grandfathers had already been ruled out—but there were other Dawes family members who might have owned such a piece. I just did not know who they were yet.

In the meantime, I gave my mother a copy of the online appraisal to add to the one she had gotten in 1973 by an antique dealer in San Francisco. Without any details of the family history, that appraiser had estimated the value at between $5,500 and $6,500, so she was delighted to see the higher numbers.

With my investigator cap now sitting tightly upon my head, I wondered what would it take to develop the "chain of custody" for George's secretary, a simple inquiry or a full-blown investigation? Most investigative agencies do preliminary inquiries after receiving a complaint or allegation. It is a quick way to see if the information received has any merit or is worthy of investing investigative resources into it. In this case, an inquiry would require a few interviews and record checks

If I were to launch into a full investigation from the start, it would be the coldest case I ever worked, requiring enormous amounts of time, computer resources, and no doubt, cash. I was short on all three.

I decided a simple inquiry was the way to go. Once I had some findings I could reassess and decide if a full investigation was warranted or even possible.

2
The Inquiry

When I started in 2000, I did things as I was originally taught — the old-fashioned way. I created a case file using a three-ring binder, organized with labeled dividers. I dated and preserved everything I found or generated, including yellow sticky notes and scraps of paper in the file. What started as one binder eventually grew into four. As you will see, sometimes the old ways are the best.

Starting with the Basics: The Case File

A "case file" is the official folder containing every piece of information and evidence gathered during an agent's investigation. I am still a bit "old school," as the kids say. I learned this job well before computers were part of our everyday lives. Today, case files are electronic. Hard copy evidence (a.k.a. documents) is scanned and embedded into the investigative report, then uploaded and maintained in the electronic case file. Original documents are usually stored elsewhere, as long as they can be easily produced at a later date should they be needed.

Interviewing 101

Here are two important rules for interviewing:

1. **Agents should take detailed notes:** We are taught to record information obtained from interviews in a formal report that becomes part of the case file, as do the agent's interview notes.

2. **Agents should never interview family members or persons they are somehow associated with:** Doing so causes an independence and ethics issue that can easily jeopardize the entire investigation. George's secretary sat in my home along with other family items I was attached to. To hell with this rule. The investigation was already personal—very personal. I was already well beyond its boundaries.

Witness #1: Ann Watts

Aside from the complicating fact that she was my mother, Ann Watts was an excellent witness, in my opinion: She knew George Dawes personally for almost thirty years. She visited and dined with the man every couple of months. She was well aware of George's finances and moral composition, having routinely received his monthly expenditure reports. George's trust in her was so complete she served as his power of attorney, a role usually reserved for family members, to help him with his finances and healthcare decisions in his final years. And, of course, it was also why George chose her to care for and maintain his secretary and the rest of the Dawes Collection.

I had grown up hearing various snippets of information describing how my mother and George met. If I put them all together, her story went something like this:

> Shortly after the end of World War II, I was barely eighteen and lived in Woodland, the county seat for Yolo County, California. Yolo was a small farming community outside Sacramento. I was finishing my senior year of high school and working in the county courthouse as a clerk. George (sixty-two at the time) was an auditor working for an accounting firm located in San Francisco. He

was given an assignment to audit a program under Yolo County's authority. I was asked to assist the out-of-town visitor during his lengthy assignment. A lasting friendship developed between us.

I married Clarence Watts in 1946. Clarence, having heard me mention George's name in our conversations, insisted we invite him to our home for dinner one night. That invitation grew into many more, to include every major holiday and birthday for the next twenty-five years. That George and Clarence happened to share the same birthday added to the sense of family.

George owned a small cottage in Camp Meeker, an old logging camp near the Russian River, about an hour outside San Francisco. When he was not travelling, George lived there with his younger brother Rufus. Rufus was mentally challenged, the result of an accident with a horse when he was a young man. George always made sure there was someone around to watch over Rufus when he was gone. Clarence and I drove to Camp Meeker on weekends occasionally to visit and dine with the two brothers.

George married later in life; his wife died in 1940. Having no children, he and Rufus became the last surviving members of this one particular Dawes line, with no legal heirs to leave any assets or personal property to. George's greatest fear was that when he died the State of California would seize all of his worldly belongings during the probate process. George's family treasures, which his father had received years earlier from his family in Massachusetts, included family silver, books, jewelry, artwork, and even some furniture. Most of these treasures were well over a hundred and fifty years old, including George's most cherished piece, an eighteenth-century mahogany secretary made in Boston before the Revolutionary War. To ensure their care and survival, George did a most remarkable thing: knowing of my love and appreciation for antiques, he entrusted me with his collection. George believed that these items would be safe with me, and he could at least enjoy seeing them whenever he visited our home.

I had no problem with this arrangement. Clarence, on the other hand, never liked the secretary. He saw no difference between an antique and an old piece of furniture ready to be thrown out and he could never imagine something that big and dark sitting in our home. The exterior finish had been slightly damaged in a fire at George's residence years earlier. We paid to have the piece refinished and when doing so, I requested a slightly lighter colored varnish. While its new appearance satisfied my husband's complaint, he still swore at it every time we moved due to its size and weight.

Rufus died in 1960 and, as George grew older, I did more than just safeguard the Dawes Collection: I watched over George as well. George maintained his steadfast regiment until suffering a severe stroke in 1972. I arranged for him to be admitted to an acceptable nursing facility where he died several months later, just two weeks shy of his eighty-eighth birthday. I took care of his funeral arrangements, making sure he had a proper burial next to Rufus in the local Masonic Cemetery.

My mother's story clearly explained how the secretary was transferred from George to her but offered no information about its previous owners other than George's father. I needed more details. It was time to treat my mother as I would any other witness. I sent her a string of thought-provoking questions like, "When did George's father receive the secretary?" and "How was it sent?"

Her responses surprised me; I was suddenly hearing details never told before. She recalled George telling her of the time when he, as a child, and his father went to the boat docks of San Francisco to receive the shipment of heirlooms from their family in Boston, many of which George had entrusted to her.

"Who sent the shipment?" I asked.

"Family," she said, her one-word answer dousing the flame of my excitement. "Family" was not a name I could use to grow our tiny list of custodians.

Now deeply rooted in my investigator role, I asked her for more details. To my surprise and delight, she found original newspaper clippings: obituaries for two Dawes family members. Though confused by their names and dates of death, she gave me copies of the obituaries. They were for a Mary E. Dawes who died in 1886, and a George Greenleaf Dawes who died in 1899. The names meant nothing to me either, but they were something to look into.

And my mother's efforts did not stop there. As is common with witnesses, given enough time to think about a past incident, multiple memories resurfaced in vivid detail. My request broke the dam and her memories began to flow.

Another email stated,

> In the time I knew him I never got to where I could ask him anything about his personal life. It would only come out in bits and parts and now I do not remember the important facts. It seems to me that his father was a Navy man. I do not know how long. His father must have died when George was a very young man and it does seem that there may have been an aunt that he looked up to as I real-ly don't remember him saying

much about his father. He did on an occasion or two
mention the disappearance of his mother.

This was all useful information but still did not provide me
with any new custodians. Meanwhile, among the personal
Dawes family items I now maintained, I discovered an old leather
billfold with "Richard Cranch Dawes, July 1898" embossed in
gold lettering on the inside pouch. A small white envelope about
the size of a business card hid inside one of the flaps, with
"Richard Cranch Dawes, Born July 16th 1838, died Dec. 2nd
1898" written across the front. This was the first time I had seen
Richard's date of death. The billfold was obviously a birthday gift
to commemorate his sixtieth birthday. I am sure no one expected
Richard to die just five months later when George was only
fourteen years old.

My mother's memories of her conversations with George
were proving to be valid and extremely helpful. With this latest
information about Richard, I could now narrow down the period
when "family" might have shipped the items to Richard in San
Francisco. Given this timeline of events, I estimated they had
arrived sometime between 1889 — when George would have been
at least five years old and able to recall such an event — and 1898,
the year Richard died.

A third email followed, and it contained even more interesting information:

> Regarding the Secretary: It was damaged at the time it
> was brought to California. Restoration work was done
> at the end of the 1800s — both workman and materials
> were of the best available. The wood was matched from
> the woods out of the Boston area. It had been used by
> George as two separate pieces since the ceilings in the
> houses would not allow for its height setup. The top was

placed on a long narrow table and used as a bookcase on its own. Then, in the late 1940s, George did have a house fire which caused additional damage — smoke and heat. The heat caused a great deal of checking in the finish, which is why we had it refinished.

In a fraud case, there is no better evidence than a statement made by a witness or, better yet, the subject, written in their own words and handwriting, admitting to what they did and how they did it. During my career, I took hundreds of written statements from subjects and witnesses. With all this added information my mother was providing, I realized I needed a written statement from her, something in addition to her emails that would document some of the important details of her story. Most importantly, it needed to mention the transfer of ownership of George's secretary from George to her. She obligingly typed out a one-page statement, signed her name, and dated it.

That was the year 2000. Who would have known that twenty years later she would suffer from dementia, no longer able to recall the transfer with any great detail? Thankfully, her best memories were well documented and preserved.

Over the years, and as this case sat in cold storage numerous times, I completely forgot about her statement and emails. When I began writing this report, I rediscovered these documents buried deep within one of the binders. Her information gave me surprising answers to a number of lingering questions that had surfaced much later in the investigation and which, at the time, I could not find answers to.

Fortunately, being old school, that statement lives on inside the case file along with the hard copies of her emails. This practice proved to be more valuable than I could ever imagine as, eight years later, I lost all electronic access to any previous emails, my mother's included, when I changed email providers.

Sometimes the old ways are the best.

Witness #2: George Dawes

Who else could serve as a credible witness for this investigation?

I knew George and had personally witnessed his relationship with my mother in later years, but he had given her the secretary well before I was born so I cannot attest to the facts as my mother described them. Aside from being the self-appointed investigator on the case, my observations over the years were seen through the eyes of a young girl whose main memories were those of receiving a dollar bill from George every time he visited and a special gift at Christmas.

Sadly, I do not recall having any in-depth conversations with George. But my mother did, and he had related his memory of being with his father at the San Francisco docks when he was a young boy. In the eyes of the law, my mother's account would be considered "hearsay" and inadmissible in court, but for this report I made an exception, since she was so intimately assoc-iated with him prior to his death. For now, it was useful lead information that might yet be verified by other sources later.

If I could bring George back to life for just one day, I would sit him down for an exceptionally long adult conversation (our first) and I would use some of my advanced interviewing techniques to see if I could break through his wall of silence about his family. Who knows what I might learn?

However, even without those coveted details, George was still an exceptionally good witness. By serving as the custodian of record for his family's books, records, and artifacts, he kept the chain of custody intact. He may not have known, or cared to share, all the stories associated with each relic, but he had meticulously stored and maintained them. I had no doubt I would find a gem or two buried within this collection. Something that might even surprise George.

Record Checks: Hard Copy vs. Electronic

In 2000, Ancestry.com was in its developmental stage. Other free online genealogical websites were also available but the accessible information was somewhat limited. I decided to use the many old books in the Dawes Collection to explore additional genealogical leads.

As a starting point, I referred to the Holland book like my mother had but this time just focusing on the lineage of George's grandfather, George Minot Dawes (1802–1871). The elder George had married Mary E. Greenleaf (1806–1886) in 1827. Their children were Nancy Cranch Dawes (who had died as an infant), Mary E. (Dawes) Mitchell (1829–1870), George Greenleaf Dawes (1832–1899), Richard Cranch Dawes (1838–1898), Ambrose Dawes (1843–1912) and Rufus Dawes (1850–1852).

Two of these names immediately caught my eye and sparked an interest: the original obituary clippings my mother found within the collection of Dawes items she kept were about Mary E. Dawes and George Greenleaf Dawes. According to the Dawes family tree, found in the Holland book, these were obituaries for George's grandmother (bestower of George's birthday cup) and one of his uncles. Both were buried in a family plot at Hancock Cemetery in Quincy, Massachusetts.

As I dug deeper into this branch of the family tree, I learned exciting new things. According to the Holland book, Richard

Dawes (George's father) married Charlotte Ann Howe in 1870. They had a daughter, Mary Nantie Dawes, born in San Francisco in 1871. She had died three years later. The Holland book was published in 1878, six years before George was born. I remembered my mother telling me once that George's mother's name was Emma. That meant Emma was Richard's second wife and begged a new question: what happened to Charlotte Howe?

Welcome to the world of investigations. As much as agents want to stay focused and on course, we are constantly bombarded with other baffling information that can easily pull our attention in other directions, away from the more important matters at hand. We refer to these as "rabbit holes." Should an investigator jump into one of these holes or not? (More on this dilemma later.)

I turned next to one of the other old books in the collection, *A History of Old Braintree and Quincy*, by William S. Pattee, MD, also published in 1878. In it, I came across a picture of a painting of an old farmhouse that looked remarkably similar to the graphite drawing by Christopher P. Cranch that I had grown up seeing on my mother's wall. The house had been built in Quincy by Lewis Vassall in 1735, and James Virchild had bought the home at auction in 1749. Some years later, around 1790, Richard Cranch, a watchmaker, took up residence, and his son-in-law John Greenleaf bought it after Cranch died in 1811. The house became known as the Cranch Greenleaf House.

Now excited to see a direct reference to my graphite drawing, I focused more on the house itself rather than the line of people who had lived in it. I was now suffering from another common disease shared by many fraud investigators: "tunnel vision." This routinely occurs when investigators get too fixated on one particular lead or finding, which invariably makes us miss other key pieces of information that are right in front of us at the same time. So even though I was starting to see the Cranch and Greenleaf names turn up in interesting places, their significance to my inquiry escaped my attention (and notes) completely.

Cranch Greenleaf House (source unknown)

From Dr. Pattee's book I learned the home had been physically moved from School Street to Water Street after the family moved out in 1856 or '57. I wondered if this old house could still be standing, preserved by some historical association. I sent an inquiry to the Quincy Historical Society. I also requested information about Hancock Cemetery in hopes of identifying other Dawes family members buried there.

The historical society's response came a few weeks later with more information than I ever expected. I sadly learned the house had been demolished years earlier — a major disappointment. On a more positive note, I received an extensive list of Dawes family members buried at Hancock Cemetery. In addition to George's grandparents and uncle, I noticed the name Harrison Dawes. A quick check in the Holland book revealed Harrison (1794–1835) was George Minot Dawes's older brother. Out of sixteen siblings, only these two brothers and their families were buried in Hancock Cemetery. Harrison's wife, Lucy (Greenleaf) Dawes (1797–1877) and his daughter, Lucy Cranch Dawes (1821–1884) were also there.

One of the biggest — and most fruitful — surprises was a copy of a letter the historical society had sent to Ms. Renee Daphne Kimball in response to her inquiry about the families of Harrison and George Minot Dawes. Who was this woman and why would she be asking about this small, insignificant branch of the Dawes family tree? I had to find out.

Fortunately, Ms. Kimball's home address was included on the letter. I wrote her a brief note explaining who I was and my connection to the Dawes family. I let her know I was curious about her interest and hoped she would contact me as soon as possible. I dropped the letter in the mail the next morning.

While at work, I could not stop wondering about this woman's interest in George's family. I ran her name through whatever Internet search engines were available at the time. To my surprise, I found a possible email address for her. Once I got home, I wasted no time copying the same note I wrote the previous day into a new email message. I hit send, wondering if she would even receive my inquiry, much less respond. Within an hour I had mail. Ten minutes later Renee and I were talking on the phone.

Nanty: The Mystery Woman

Renee was delighted to hear from me. She lived in Portland, Oregon, and explained that in 1995 she had purchased a box of old letters written between 1843 and 1870 from a local used bookstore. Most were signed by a woman named "Nanty." Renee claimed they were a living history of four families—the Cranches, Daweses, Greenleafs, and Eliots—during the intellectual heyday of Massachusetts, Virginia, and Washington, DC. She was in the process of transcribing each letter and the "cartoons" that accompanied them. It was a painstaking exercise. Renee hoped to write a mystery novel involving the women from these families. She had no idea who Nanty was but wished her identity to remain a mystery for as long as possible.

I had not seen the name "Nanty" in my research other than noticing a similarity with the middle name of Richard's young daughter, Mary Nantie Dawes. I was more than happy to provide Renee with more information about the Dawes family members and I let her know I had a copy of the Holland book. I knew I could help her identify many of the people mentioned in the letters. I told her about my quest to discover the origins of George's secretary. Perhaps something in these letters would make a solid connection.

Renee asked me to send her a photograph of George's secretary and promised to be on the lookout for any connections during the transcription process. I found myself filled with hope believing that somehow "Nanty's letters" could be the key to unlocking this cold case.

When I connected with Renee, it had been five years since

she discovered Nanty's letters. That flame of excitement she had felt during her initial review now burned low. Without a full understanding of the family connections and dynamics, the transcriptions meant little, which must have added to her frustration.

The discovery of a new source (me) who could provide insider information about this mysterious family rekindled Renee's desire to push on but, just like me, many other projects and priorities required her time and attention. I knew Nanty's letters were something she would get to eventually, just not now.

I would have to be patient and wait.

Descendants of William Dawes Who Rode Association

With little more to go on, I decided to send out one more letter. I reached out to an organization called the Descendants of William Dawes Who Rode Association, not knowing what I would find. I received an informative and personal reply from association member Margaret Hyun. Unlike George, she was a direct descendant of William Who Rode. She explained the purpose of their association was to facilitate connections among descendants of William Dawes through their newsletters and reunions, and invited me to attend one of their upcoming events. We spoke on the phone a few times and she expressed an interest in seeing George's secretary.

A visit to my house followed months later, and I took pride in showing her the first edition of the Holland book. Looking inside the front cover and seeing Richard Cranch Dawes's name on the first page, she informed me her mother also had a copy of the Holland book, found in an old used bookstore in New York City years earlier, and it too had a name written on the front page.

A few days later Margaret called to share the name written in her mother's book. She said the name, and the world stopped for a brief second as I experienced my first bizarre and unbelievable incident with this case:

"George Greenleaf Dawes," she calmly reported, sending a spine-tingling chill up and down my whole body. George's uncle! Richard Cranch Dawes's older brother. The very man whose obituary my mother had handed into my care. Out of only a hundred printed copies, what were the chances of meeting someone a hundred years after Richard's death, who owned a copy once belonging to his brother? This was the beginning of many such incidents yet to follow.

In the investigative world, reviewing old records and books can be incredibly tedious, leaving agents to wonder if their efforts are worth the time spent. Unfortunately, without any additional leads, my inquiry failed to produce enough evidence to justify opening a full investigation. By this time, I knew a bit more about George's extended family but I was no closer to identifying a family member as the owner of his secretary. Plus, my full-time profession needed my undivided attention. It was time to restock the cold storage locker and lock the door.

3

The Hiatus

Even though the inquiry was officially suspended at this point, the mystery of George's secretary somehow retained a small workspace area in a vacant cell in my brain where theories and practical solutions rarely rested. Every so often something unexpected would happen, sparking intense moments of interest and activity. Such was the case in 2002, when a short work assignment took me to Boston. I could not pass up an opportunity to do a little research about George's secretary.

With a day of annual leave at my disposal, I decided family probate records might be a good place to start, to see if members of George's immediate family had possessed a secretary when they died. Doing this in person saved me the expense of ordering and paying for copies of documents without knowing what they revealed.

Entering the Time Machine

Mary E. Dawes (George's grandmother) was living in Brookline, Massachusetts, when she died in 1886, fifteen years after her husband George Minot Dawes. If Mary Dawes left the secretary to her son Richard, I reasoned, perhaps it would be listed in these records. Brookline was in Norfolk County; the index indicated her file was available.

I was stunned by what I saw in the file the clerk delivered to my table. There, in front of me, was the original folder with all of the documents intact—original documents, not a copy in the lot.

I was looking at records created over 110 years earlier. I felt like that young girl again, inside one of those antique stores my mother dragged me into. I am now a believer in time machines; this one transported me back to 1886 as soon as I touched the first page of the document with my gloveless hand.

I discovered that Richard Cranch Greenleaf, Mary Dawes's brother, had served as the executor of her will. Unfortunately, I saw no mention of a secretary in any of the documents.

Since Mary's daughter Mary E. (Dawes) Mitchell had pre-deceased her and had no children, she left each son (George, Richard, and Ambrose) $1,583.57 (about $45,000 in today's currency). Their names appeared on the last page of the document acknowledging the disbursement and receipt of funds.

With this information, I knew George's father had travelled from his home in San Francisco to the Boston area in late 1886 or early 1887. With both parents dead, perhaps this is when he and his two brothers discussed how family belongings were to be divided. For Richard, taking possession of family items was one thing; getting them back to San Francisco would be another. His only two options would have been by ship or rail. According to my mother's emails, he chose ship, which, as this was thirty years before the Panama Canal was completed, meant the shipment had to travel around the tip of South America to get to San Francisco.

I am unfortunately not certain about the shipment date. No doubt it would have been up to Richard's brother George who still lived in the Brookline home where their parents lived until their deaths. Perhaps George shipped everything once he closed it down.

Meeting the Dawes Family

My next visit was to the Hancock Cemetery in Quincy, a thirty-minute train ride outside of Boston. As I entered the grounds through the open iron gates, I noticed the words written on the archway above the entry gate, "Dust thou art & unto dust thou shalt return." I was stepping back to another time with each unhurried stride. A variety of headstones filled the grounds, some so old the inscriptions were nothing but blurred letters. The only thing keeping me anchored to the present day was a train passing by on the tracks located at the far end of the cemetery, the area I was headed.

Then I saw it: a huge, dark, stone monument sitting solemnly in the back corner of the cemetery grounds, surrounded by smaller headstones, all enclosed within an ornate black iron fence. The inscription on the monument read, "George Minot Dawes 1802–1872," the man our George was named after. Next to George's grandfather lay his grandmother Mary E. Dawes, whose probate records I had just touched and reviewed. Additional headstones laid within this private enclosure, George Greenleaf Dawes, Mary E. (Dawes) Mitchell, Nancy Cranch Dawes, and Rufus Dawes. I was standing before George's aunts, uncles, and grandparents. As I stepped closer, a powerful, mysterious aura suddenly touched something deep inside me. Tears trickled down my cheeks. I found myself grieving over the loss of this family even though I barely knew who they were. I had just started learning about these people through their possessions and life histories. Now they all laid silent together as a family in this small grassy plot, with only their deteriorating headstones left to mark their existence. I wondered if our George had ever been here.

Just steps away, another monument caught my attention. As I approached, I could make out the name "Harrison" in the fading inscription. This marked the graves of Harrison Dawes, his wife Lucy (Greenleaf) Dawes, and their daughter Lucy Cranch Dawes. I finally realized that Lucy (Greenleaf) Dawes and Mary E. (Greenleaf) Dawes were sisters. It was quite common in their day for brothers of one family to marry sisters from another.

I returned home better informed but still no closer to learning the origin of George's secretary.

Letting the Stew Simmer

After my return, I found myself studying the photographs I took of all the headstones in the Daweses' burial area. On the stones for Lucy (Greenleaf) Dawes and her daughter Lucy, I noticed both died in Brookline, Massachusetts, like Mary E. (Greenleaf) Dawes and her husband George. I knew I had seen Brookline mentioned before, but I could not figure out where.

Brain teasers like this keep investigators up at night. My usual investigative solution for finding uncertain connections is to put an issue on a back burner and let it simmer for a while.

As usual, the practice paid off a few days later but not in the way I expected. I was sitting at George's secretary and happened to look at an old photograph my mother had left with me years earlier, of a house hidden by overgrown trees. I didn't give the photo much thought but had assumed it was a view of the Cranch Greenleaf House, taken from a different angle than the Christopher P. Cranch drawing. This time, I flipped the photo over and noticed the photographer's name. "E. R. Hills, Photographer, Brookline, Mass." Brookline? Where was Brookline located? I found a map of the Boston area and saw Brookline was about ten miles from Quincy.

The Dawes Brookline Home, circa 1860s
by E.R. Hills, Photographer, Brookline, Massachusetts

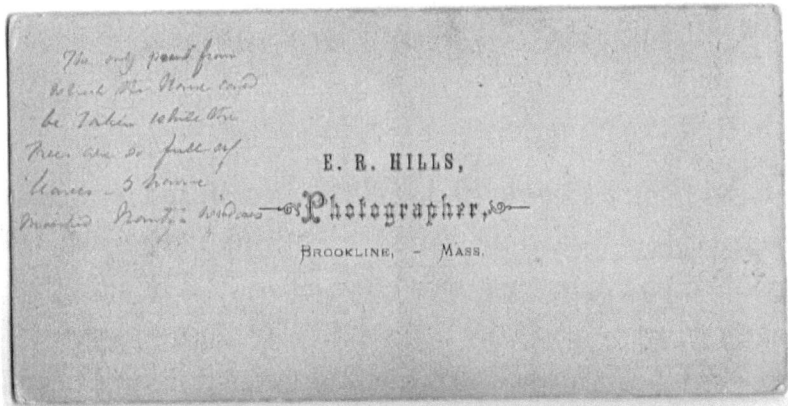

"The only point from which the home can be taken while
the trees are so full of leaves. I have marked Nanty's window."

I took a closer look at the photograph, noticing for the first time a word written in pencil under and alongside two second story windows of the house. I had to use a magnifying glass to read the handwriting. When I did, another bizarre and unbelievable incident hit with full force: "Nanty's," it read. There was also a handwritten note on the back of the picture. With magnifying glass in hand, I was able to read the following, "The only point from which the home can be taken while the trees are so full of leaves. I have marked Nanty's window." That familiar chill was making a racetrack out of my spine.

Nanty's window in the Daweses' Brookline home

Deciphering the Notation

Until now, Nanty's name had only existed in the letters Renee purchased. Now it had appeared on an item from the Dawes Collection, on an item well over 110 years old. Who was this woman named Nanty and how did she fit into George's family?

Once my heart stopped racing and I was thinking rationally again, I knew I needed to find out who lived in this home. But it was a difficult prospect with no address. I couldn't even be sure it was located in Brookline.

Luckily, the 1880 US Census had just become available online. I searched for Mary E. Dawes in Massachusetts. She was identified as the head of household in a home in Brookline. Also living in the same home was George Greenleaf Dawes (son), Lucy Cranch Dawes (niece) and Mary Murry (servant). Might either

Mary or her niece be Nanty? I failed to find any possible clues within this government record.

What about the 1870 US Census? It was also available. George M. Dawes had still been alive and listed as the head of household in the same Brookline home with the following family members: Mary E. (wife), George G. (son), Henry Mitchell (son-in-law), Mary Aiken (domestic servant), and Elizabeth Johnson (domestic servant). I found no good leads from this source either.

Even so, I could not wait to share this discovery with Renee. We had not corresponded in over a year. Needless to say, she was as surprised as I was about my Nanty sighting. I promised to send her a copy of the photo (which took a regrettably long time, due to having just transferred to another agency and traveling more than ever before).

First Glimpse of the Nanty Letters

In return, Renee finally shared two of Nanty's letters with me, the first written as a rebus — a combination of pictures and letters in place of words. For instance, a deer and a cross skull appeared as the opening greeting and meant "Dear Bones."

Who was Bones? Ah yes, another mystery to solve. Fortunately, the answer became quite obvious when I flipped the letter over. In the area reserved for the addressee "Miss Lucy C. Dawes, care of J.P Norton Esq., Lowell, Mass" was clearly written. Lucy Cranch Dawes used the nickname "Bones." I was able to decipher about 60 percent of the drawings in the letter. At the end, Nanty drew a small self-portrait, complete with pigtails and an over-sized mouth, as a signature. As childish as it appeared, I now had an image of Nanty to add to my file.

The first Nanty's rebus I deciphered

January 9th 1843

(Dear Bones),

(I) don't believe anyone has told *(---)* about *(---)*'s *(letter)*, she arrived whole length in New York Wednesday morning and will stay with Mrs Charles during the absence of *(---)* say about a week; she was not very *(sick)* on board the *(ship)*; did not say a word about *(---)* or his wife, suppose they continued on to the *(Capital)*. *(Uncle Richard)* sends his love to *(---)* and thinks she can't do better than come back with *(---)*. Mr *(Apple)*ton has *(sailed)* for Cuba; and the *(whale)* is staying with her *(mother)*; the *(sisters)* at their uncle *(---)* *(Apple)*ton's in Dorchester.

My *(---)* has gone off my *(---)*. The *(reverend)* is going to preach, to preach at the *(church)*. And now *(I)* must *(be)(ring)* this *(letter)(to)* a close and *(ass)*ure *(you)* *(I)* am *(yours)* ways *(Nanty)*

Renee shared her thoughts as to why family members used nicknames. During this era, especially in families of English descent, it was common to name one's first, second, or even third born child after parents and grand-parents. With families ranging from eight to fifteen children, the repetition of names in second and third gen-erations must have created incredible confusion during family gatherings. Can you imagine what would have happened when calling out for George, Mary, or Lucy at a Dawes Christmas dinner? Nicknames had to be the sol-ution. I liked Renee's theory.

The second letter, dated February 16, 1869, Renee had labeled "14Henrywife69." She had tried to identify people mentioned in the letter and placed comments in her tran-scription copy. I noticed a few familiar first names but, again, they were the same names these families used overand over in each generation, George, Richard, Mary, Lucy. I had no idea who was who nor did the contents ring any bells. So much for this small spurt of carrot-dangling entertainment.

Looking for a Needle in a Haystack

By 2003 my travel schedule had eased a bit, leaving me with a few minutes to think about my inquiry once again. I was by now a constant follower of *Antiques Roadshow* and taking notice of the various auction houses that provided appraisers to the show. As a long shot, I decided to reach out to Skinner, Inc., a group of auctioneers and appraisers located in Boston, to see if they might be able to provide additional information about George's secretary. Skinner referred me to Brock Jobe, professor of American decorative arts at the University of Delaware and Winterthur Museum and the "go-to guy" when it came to eighteenth-century secretaries. My witness list had expanded to include a new category: the expert witness.

Expert witnesses provide testimony at trials based on their expertise and extensive experience within a particular field of study. More importantly, as subject experts, these individuals often provide agents with advice on how to tackle matters outside the agent's own knowledgebase, saving time and resources.

I sent Mr. Jobe an email describing George's secretary and my connection to the Dawes family. I asked if he was aware of any known family pieces that might match mine and waited patiently for his reply. His response did not disappoint. Mr. Jobe said he was well-aware of the secretary owned by Colonel Dawes. He thought George's secretary was an intriguing piece, similar to Boston area furniture of the 1740s, 50s, and 60s.

My first real OSOD (Oh shit, oh dear) discovery of the case! Mr. Jobe's expert opinion not only substantiated the allegation (that George's secretary was made in Boston sometime prior to the Revolutionary War) but it pinpointed a more precise age range not previously known.

This, however, was the easier of the two allegations to prove. One down, one to go.

Mr. Jobe's email continued, "I do suggest that you go over the piece very carefully, looking for any inscriptions, numbers, letters, etc. Often cabinetmakers marked their work in chalk or sometimes graphite. The marks might be nothing more than a series of numbers or letters, but they can be clues to the original maker. If you discover anything, please let me know."

He also suggested reviewing probate inventories and wills in hopes of finding a reference to a desk and bookcase but warned, "This is needle-in-a-haystack work and at the end of the day you cannot be certain that the desk and bookcase listed in the probate inventory is really your piece."

I followed up with a return email thanking him for the information and his suggestions and let him know I had already reviewed probate records for Mary (Greenleaf) Dawes with negative results. Then I asked about the use of secretaries during that particular period.

"Desk and bookcases were rare in the eighteenth century," he responded. "They were favored by merchants and clergymen and considered a sign of wealth and learning. Typically, they were kept in parlors but not always the best parlor. I find them listed frequently in the second or family parlor (as opposed to the most formal parlor) of estate inventories of the late eighteenth century. I also find reference to them in dining rooms."

This was all extremely insightful and I added all of Mr. Jobe's information to the case file. However, career demands once again pulled me away from my newfound hobby. It would be another three years before I could find time to play with more theories and investigative leads.

4
The Investigation

When I retired early from the profession I was born to do, I found it difficult to adapt to the world outside of law enforcement. As one should, I had a list of projects lined up, ready to fill all those hours that were once dictated by my career. It only took six months to complete everything on my "to-do-after-retiring" list. Boredom quickly set in. I missed my office; more notably, I missed doing investigations and the demanding yet challenging thought process I was accustomed to that kept my mind active and alive.

When I sent Renee the next update, she responded a few months later advising she was still committed to ongoing projects and no closer to working on her book than before. After three long years of being sidelined, thoughts of the Dawes inquiry resurfaced, reminding me how much I enjoyed working on the case when time allowed.

Now, with nothing but time on my hands, I pulled the box containing George's personal family treasures and my carefully created case files out of the cold storage locker and reacquainted myself with the dated materials I had once collected.

Among the first documents I looked at was Renee's 14Henrywife69 letter. Even after a three-year hiatus, I stumbled right into another bizarre and unbelievable incident, this time with extra chills running up and down my spine. I had been so fascinated with the "Dear Bones" letter Renee sent with this one

I apparently never went back to take a closer look and I had missed these simple connections:

- The letter, addressed to Lucy Dawes, who was then living in Washington, DC, had not been signed but Renee was quite sure, based on the handwriting, it was one of Nanty's letters.

- Assuming so, Nanty wrote about various activities involving members of her family and mentioned each by name.

- Though they were the same common first names I had seen before, they all suddenly jumped off the page and fell into place, like branches on the family tree.

There was no doubt in my mind: I knew Nanty's true identity.

Nanty was Mary E. (Dawes) Mitchell, George's aunt. The same woman whose grave marker I stared at as it laid next to George and Mary Dawes in their family plot. The same woman who made the young girl's stitch sampler now hanging on a bedroom wall in my house with "Mary E. Dawes, Aged 11 years, 1840" sewn into the fabric.

What were the chances of finding personal letters written by George's aunt, a woman who died fourteen years before he was born? And in Portland, Oregon, of all places! I wanted to get on a plane and fly there immediately, to finally meet Renee and to see the full collection of Nanty letters firsthand. Renee had only shared a few choice examples of these letters up until this point. What could the rest of the collection tell me about George's family, or better yet, George's secretary? Unfortunately, I had promised Renee years earlier that I would not reveal Nanty's identity should I figure it out. It felt like she wanted to experience the joy of that discovery herself. What else could I do with this new surge of excitement and energy?

My investigative juices, now ignited into full power mode, left me wondering what else I might have missed in past reviews. I decided to push forward even without Renee and Nanty's letters. It was time to open a full investigation.

Identifying the Players

My approach to this case was the same as any other complex fraud investigation. I needed to identify all the players (family members) and develop an extensive link chart (family tree) showing relationships between each person. The Holland book was a wonderful guide for the Dawes family members but, as I soon discovered, their personal associations bled over into other family lines, most belonging to the Cranches and Greenleafs, names that had surfaced in past documents but I had failed to notice. Who were these people? I subscribed to Ancestry.com, to discover their personal histories and how they connected to one another.

Much to my benefit, these families and family members were all from Massachusetts, a state that has been collecting and maintaining meticulous public records since the British invasion. I was amazed at how much historic information I could access from a non-law enforcement database: dates and places of birth, dates of death and marriages, parents' names, spouses, children, wills, and probate records. Once I learned how to search properly it was all at my fingertips.

As a fraud investigator, managing this flood of added information was an effortless process. I created a background form for each new person and family member identified, containing numerous blocks, all labeled by category, such as date and place of birth, date and place of death, parents, siblings, and so on, that could be expanded as needed. Filling in each block showed me an overview of a person's life. An empty box indicated the need for additional research. I also inserted any found photographs of the family member at the top of the sheet. By the time I was finished, the only remaining box on each form was the one reserved for the title of the case — the main suspect — who had yet to be identified.

As my obsession for identifying the family member who might have once owned George's secretary intensified, I began to wonder if the term "family" might extend beyond the Dawes line. I decided to research George's grandmother's ancestry, looking first at her parents and grandparents. If I applied the same theory my mother had used years earlier while searching out Colonel Dawes, I would be looking for an individual alive during the Revolutionary War. John Greenleaf (1763–1848), Mary (Greenleaf) Dawes's father had been alive during the war but a bit too young and he had also been blinded as a young boy. His father, William Greenleaf (1725–1803), was a successful merchant who, serving as the Suffolk County Sheriff in July 1776, had read out the Declaration of Independence from the balcony of Boston's Old State House. A person in his position (and a merchant) could very well have owned a secretary — but did he?

What took my mother months to research on the colonel now only took me a few hours, using the Internet. William Green-leaf had in fact owned a secretary, which was now in the hands of a private party.

There was one more line to follow that led to an unexpected OSOD ("Oh shit, oh dear!") discovery: Mary (Greenleaf) Dawes's mother was Lucy (Cranch) Greenleaf, Richard and Mary (Smith)

Cranch's daughter! This shocked me to my core, as my dumb-founded brain finally made the obvious connections between George and the Cranch family. The clues were so transparent: George's own father, Richard Cranch Dawes, was named after John Adams's best friend, Richard Cranch. Richard and his wife, Mary Cranch, sister of Abigail Adams, were George's great-great-grand-parents. Of greater importance, this meant George was actually Abigail Adams's great-great-grandnephew.

I was awestruck. All those years this quiet little old man had visited our home and sat at our holiday dinner table, my family never knowing about his impressive ancestral connections.

Cranches and Greenleafs and Daweses (Oh My!)

Richard Cranch was born in England and emigrated to America in 1746. A watchmaker by trade, he was also an extensive reader of books and a learned man, especially in theology. He even received an honorary degree from Harvard University. I thought back to Brock Jobe's description of the characteristics of men who owned secretaries in the eighteenth century. Cranch fit his description to a tee. Plus, Cranch was a simple man, a characteristic reflected in the style of George's secretary. But more importantly, one big question remained: had Cranch ever owned one?

This time my hurried Internet research failed to find any connection to or mention of Cranch and a secretary. No museum or auction house reported ever owning or selling a secretary belonging to Cranch. I queried the Massachusetts Probate Records database and found a record for Richard Cranch in Norfolk County, where he died in 1811 while still living in the Quincy family home. A will was on file but not available online.

Richard Cranch, circa late 1700s

I wasted no time filling out a request form and enclosing my check for $45. I also included requests for documents about John Greenleaf, Mary (Dawes) Mitchell, and Lucy Cranch Dawes along with another check for $135. The wait was on.

In the meantime, I continued to gather information on other family members. I finally began to understand how the Cranch, Greenleaf, and Dawes families had all came to know one another.

Richard and Mary Cranch had three children:

- *Daughter Elizabeth, the oldest, born in 1763,* moved to Weymouth when she married the Reverend Jacob Norton.

- *Daughter Lucy, their middle child, born in 1767,* amidst much family debate, married William Greenleaf's son John who was blinded as a young child. John purchased the Cranch family home after Richard and Mary died in 1811; he and Lucy remained there for the rest of their lives.

- *Son William, the youngest, born in 1769,* became an attorney and — with help from his well-placed uncle, President John Adams — was appointed as a judge to the US District Court in Washington, DC. He married William Greenleaf's daughter Nancy.

John and Lucy had seven children: Daughters Lucy, born in 1797, and Mary, born in 1806, were extremely close, even with a nine-year age gap between them. Each would find love with one of Colonel Thomas Dawes's grandsons, Lucy with Harrison and Mary with George Minot. Harrison became an auctioneer for a company in Baltimore, Maryland, sometime before 1820. In 1827, George and Mary joined Harrison and Lucy in Baltimore.

Of the five Greenleaf sons, only Richard and William lived beyond the age of 27. Richard became a notably successful merchant in Boston. William relocated to Washington, DC, and served as a secretary to President John Quincy Adams during his administration, later remaining in DC as a clerk for the US government.

By 1832, the aging John and Lucy Greenleaf found themselves needing additional assistance with their home and personal care. Mary and George returned to Quincy from Baltimore to take on the responsibility and moved into the Cranch Green-leaf House with their young daughter Mary (Nanty).

In 1835, tragedy struck the Dawes family: Harrison Dawes died unexpectantly, shortly after the birth of his sixth child. Lucy, now a widow, packed up her children and moved back to Quincy, joining Mary and George and her parents in the Cranch Greenleaf House. The 1840 US Census reports fifteen individuals living in the home that year.

Charting the Data

By the time I had finally finished my research, the collection of background forms included four generations of Dawes, Cranch, and Greenleaf family members. As I became more engrossed with the details of their lives, I could easily see how deeply these families had depended on one another over the years. Without modern-day social security benefits or senior living facilities, each generation cared for the preceding one as they aged or became sick and incapacitated.

With so many names in the mix, I needed a visual represent-ation of my data, to keep track of these various family groups and to see how each was associated with the other. In the inves-tigative world, I had routinely accomplished this using a "link chart," which I created to show associations between targets, their associates, and the companies they did business with. In this case, companies were not at issue so I decided a simple family tree would serve as the perfect link chart, and Ancestry's program made it easy to build.

But once I had entered every family member into the pro-gram, the final chart had too many crossed lines. With so many marriages between Dawes, Cranch, and Greenleaf families, plus more children added with each new generation, it was impossible to make sense of the final product. So I settled for two scaled-down charts, one for Colonel Thomas Dawes and his wife Hannah Blake (see appendix A) and one for Richard Cranch and his wife Mary Smith (appendix B).

My third link chart was for the union of the two Dawes brothers (Harrison and George Minot) with the two Greenleaf sisters (Lucy and Mary; see appendix C) and their offspring. As mentioned, the 1840 US Census reported fifteen people living in the Cranch Greenleaf House. Until 1850, the census only provided the name of the head of household; all other family members were only identified by sex and age group. So the chart in appendix C serves as my best guess as to who those family members might have been.

What is not illustrated in these charts is the fact that the Dawes brothers and the Greenleaf sisters were also first cousins: Harrison and George's father, Judge Thomas Dawes, was married to Margaret Greenleaf, sister of John Greenleaf, Lucy and Mary's father.

Tackling the Timeline

Another helpful tool used in complex fraud investigations is a timeline documenting events and activities. Simple timelines are often used in general crime cases to establish an individual's whereabouts before, during, and after a crime, which may help to prove or disprove a suspect's stated alibi. In my investigations, I often used multidimensional timelines, to show ongoing activities of numerous people at the same time. When a suspect's activities are lined up with others involved in a criminal act, their involvement may suddenly become quite obvious. I have even located assets purchased with the proceeds of a crime using this technique.

In this case, my focus was finding the possible path of George's secretary should Richard Cranch have once owned one. I began my timeline with Richard and Mary Cranch in 1790 when the couple reportedly moved into the Virchild House—which later became known as the Cranch House—and added family members who stayed in the Quincy area throughout their life-time. Lucy Cranch Greenleaf was Richard and Mary's only child to remain. Of further interest to me were John and Lucy's children, sons Richard and William, and two daughters, Lucy and Mary. I continued to add family members until the timeline ended in 1972 with the death of our George.

Each member's place on the timeline began the year they were born. Using the appropriate year block, I then documented when each married and died. As I was interested in illustrating where these family members lived during their lives, I inserted the name of the city in the block corresponding to the year they first lived there. To make the chart even more interesting, I developed a color code for each city and shaded each block with the appropriate color. For example, I used a tan color for time lived in the Cranch Greenleaf House, blue for Washington, DC, pink for Brookline. I was curious to see if a possible path for George's secretary might emerge.

When my timeline was complete, I could see the lifetime movements of twenty-four family members over a span of almost 180 years. With this visual aid in front of me, it was time to develop a practical investigative theory as to where Richard Cranch's secretary might have gone (should he have owned one) after his death. As I studied the pattern of tan-colored blocks (time spent living in the Cranch Greenleaf House) sprinkled across the chart, I began to see a pathway emerge involving a handful of key people.

The Cranch Greenleaf House had remained in the family's possession from at least 1790 through 1856 or '57. After Richard and Mary Cranch died in 1811 (just one day apart), John and Lucy (Cranch) Greenleaf purchased the home and moved in. Their children all lived in the house at various times. Their two daughters eventually returned as adults, Mary with her husband and family in or around 1831, and Lucy as a widow with her six children in 1835. After John and Lucy Greenleaf both died, the two sisters and their families remained in the home until the late 1850s, when each moved into separate residences in Melrose, twenty miles north of Quincy.

The chart supported my theory that the secretary had been physically located in the Cranch Greenleaf House as early as 1790, under the care and ownership of Richard Cranch. And it had no doubt remained in the house until 1856 or '57, cared for first by Lucy (Cranch) Greenleaf and then her daughters, Mary and Lucy Dawes.

But where had George's secretary gone when the family left the home? If it had ended up with Richard Cranch Dawes, George's father, then Mary (Greenleaf) Dawes (see appendix D) must have taken possession of it.

This was a logical theory but I was getting ahead of myself. I still needed to prove Richard Cranch had once owned a secretary.

Nanty, in the Flesh

During this process, Renee sent me two cartoon drawings from the Nanty letters. The woman knew how to push my emotional buttons with her selection of shared drawings. The first, entitled,

"Final Scene in the Front Parlor at Cranch Hall" depicted the day in 1856 or '57 when the two Dawes families moved out of the Cranch Greenleaf House (or so I thought for the next thirteen years).

Although the drawing did not provide any evidence to identify our mystery family member, it qualified as a true bizarre and unbelievable incident. How often do you get to peek into the past, over 150 years earlier, to observe a day in the life of people you have come to know and care about?

As I stared into this scene I felt like I was on a surveillance once again, this time carefully watching through an open window from outside the Cranch Greenleaf House in hopes of identifying other family members and learning about their lives and activities. Although their comments appeared written in bubbles above their heads, I swear I could hear each word as if spoken aloud.

Woman (far left): *"Here's wrapping papers enough, I should think but I'll bring a barrel full from the library in case you want more."*

Sarah (domestic): *"Indeed, indeed Miss Nanty, I hope you don't think them's the last of 'em. There's three more on the landing up there, and one in the Judge's room besides these here."*

Nanty (middle): *"Sarah you pack 'em in and I'll wrap 'em up. Here's one for husband and I saw ___ the girls."*

Woman (far right): *"Why don't you put in that green one of Margie Brooks for a nest egg, it looks as if it must be the mother of a small brood in the course of the day."*

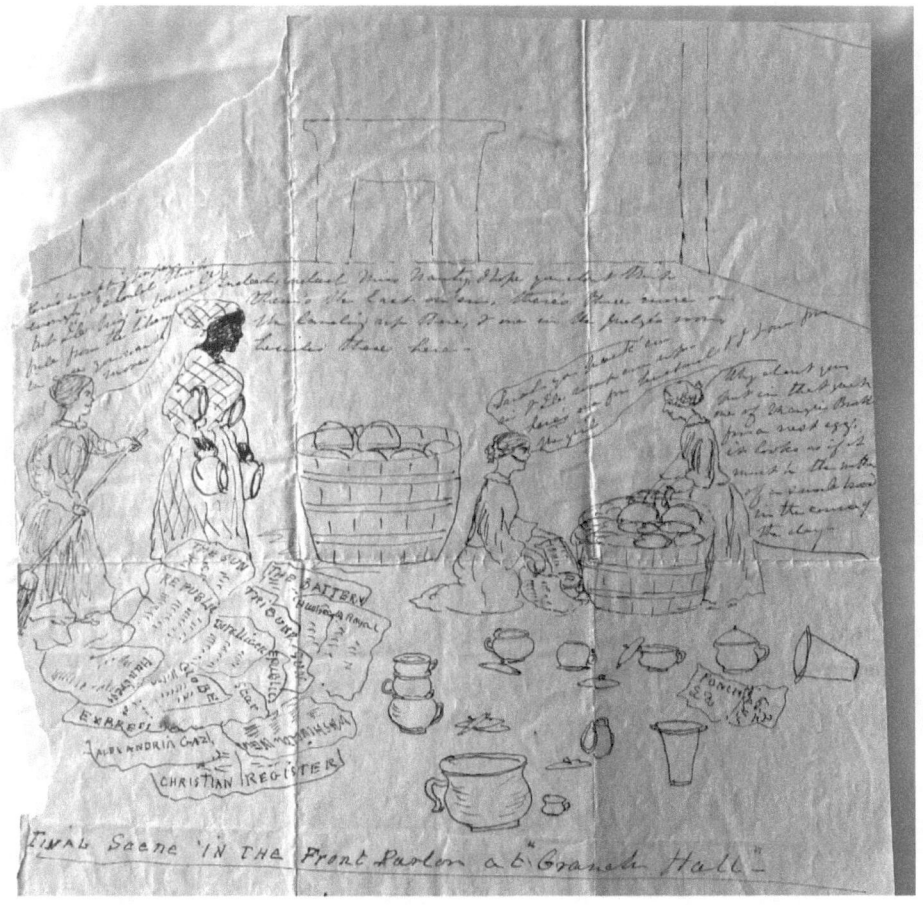

"Final Scene in the Front Parlor at Cranch Hall"

In the drawing, the second woman to the right addresses the woman sitting on the floor as "Miss Nanty." I already knew Nanty was Mary E. (Dawes) Mitchell, but now I had my first image of Nanty as an adult. The pigtails were gone but her oversized smile was still obvious. She had a defined shape and a recognizable face. Nanty replied to the woman, calling her "Sarah." At this point, it was only a partial ID for Sarah, but more than I had before. Who were these other women in the drawing? Possibly Nanty's mother or her Aunt Lucy. Perhaps one of her cousins.

I pulled up a copy of the 1855 Massachusetts Census from the Internet for clues, which identified who was still living in the home just prior to the family moving out. Listed under George Minot Dawes were his wife Mary E. and their sons, George G., Richard C., and Ambrose. Their daughter, Mary (Nanty), had married Henry Mitchell in 1854 and was no longer living in the family home. The family of Lucy G. Dawes followed, listing Lucy and her children, Lucy C., Harrison J., and Margaret C. The final entry was Agnes H. (age 1), Lucy's granddaughter. The name Sarah did not appear anywhere. The Daweses did not own slaves but finding any kind of information for a free black woman during those years is extremely difficult.

Family scene, probably in the back yard of the
Cranch Greenleaf House, circa 1845

The second drawing Renee sent was untitled, though I assumed it was a scene in the back yard of the Cranch Greenleaf House. Given her wide smile, it was not hard to identify Nanty as the young girl standing to the far right with her back against the wall. She appeared to be much younger in this scene than in the previous one. I thought the three boys in the yard were likely her brothers, George (age 12), Richard (age 8), and Ambrose (age 2), and the tall gentleman next to the tree likely John Greenleaf, Nanty's grandfather. I deduced that the old woman collecting water from the pump was most likely John's wife and Nanty's grandmother Lucy. I could not identify the baby in John's arms or the woman sitting to Nanty's left. Lucy died in 1846 and John in 1848, leaving me to believe Nanty drew this scene around 1845.

Filling in the Title Block

These discoveries helped pass the time as I waited anxiously for a response from the Massachusetts Probate Office. A large envelope finally arrived in the mail a few weeks later. The world stood still for a brief moment, my mind filled with doubtful anticipation. I had been playing with this project for the past six years, eager to find a key piece of evidence linking George's secretary to its historic owner. What if there was nothing in these documents to support my new theory about Richard Cranch? What would be my next step?

I took a deep breath, opened the packet, and pulled out a set of neatly copied documents. On the top, a copy of Richard Cranch's original handwritten will. Behind this document were copies of probate records filed with Norfolk County following Cranch's death in October 1811. Wasting no time, I flipped to the inventory of his possessions. There, on the second line in black and white, were the words I had been waiting so long to see: "1 Desk & Bookcase $10." In other words, Richard Cranch had indeed owned a secretary:

Norfolk County Probate Court, partial inventory of
Richard Cranch estate, December 1811

This was the evidence I had been looking for. My long-awaited OSOD discovery (with outburst) was followed by a happy dance around my study, sadly without any spectators. If I had still carried them, I would have been reaching for my handcuffs to arrest Richard Cranch or, at the very least, pick the man up for further questioning.

However, this was not a criminal offense so no arrest was imminent. It was time for celebration, but only momentarily. As the probate records clearly indicated, Cranch owned a secretary but was it the same one that now sat so impressively in my study? A lot could have happened over the next 200 years.

If I could not make the arrest or even enjoy a well-deserved celebration, at least this confirmation gave me enough cause for inserting Richard Cranch's name into the title block of my investigation. Cranch met all the criteria I was looking for in a target. More importantly, to my knowledge no one knew the whereabouts of the secretary mentioned in his probate inventory.

From this point forward, I would be proving Richard Cranch.

Dividing Family Heirlooms

Something else had started to bother me. The name "Margaret Dawes" was suddenly making its presence known as I was working on the link charts and reviewing census documents. Margaret Dawes was the youngest daughter of Harrison and Lucy Dawes. Why was her name so familiar?

I took out the case file and started reviewing documents and past correspondence. In the 2002 AuctionWatch.com appraisal for George's secretary, I noticed an additional comment from the appraiser regarding the Adams/Cranch japanned high chest that had sold at auction by Sotheby's in 1999 for $1.6 million: It had descended in the family of Abigail Adams's sister, Mary Cranch, to Margaret Cranch Dawes of St. Louis in 1876.

For the first time I realized Margaret Dawes "of St. Louis" was actually the same Margaret Dawes "of Quincy," a cousin to Nanty, George, Richard, and Ambrose Dawes who had grown up in the Cranch Greenleaf House since she was a toddler. She had married Lyman Ripley in 1858 and moved to St. Louis.

I needed to find out more about the path of this japanned high chest so I recontacted Sotheby's to see if they had any additional information. Sotheby's Associate Erik Gronning, another expert witness for my list, forwarded me a copy of the auction item information sheet. In addition to a detailed descript-tion of the chest, the sheet provided the item's full provenance, from John Adams to Mary Cranch to Lucy (Cranch) Greenleaf, to Lucy (Greenleaf) Dawes, to Margaret, and so on, for another five generations. This pathway aligned perfectly with my theory about George's secretary with just one exception: the high chest had gone to Mary's sister Lucy. If you think about it, it seems only logical that each sister would receive a piece of furniture once belonging to their grandparents. Lucy received the high chest, Mary the secretary.

In my correspondence with Erik, I mentioned my connection with the Dawes family. He asked for a photograph of George's secretary and a few weeks later I received his evaluation. He believed it was made around 1755, which added a more precise year to the evidence and the opinion of other experts who had similarly opined before him. However, he was not able to iden-tify the "very skilled as of yet unknown" cabinetmaker, based on the limited history I provided, but (conservatively) estimated the secretary's value between $40,000 and $80,000. That old familiar chorus of "Provenance" was singing to me again—with an additional value of $30,000 to $60,000 should I be able to prove the family connection. "Provenance" was now becoming my fav-orite tune!

It was now December 2007. Armed with this latest infor-mation, I decided to recontact Brock Jobe, just to see if he might have anything new for my investigative plan (or lack thereof). Brock advised he had been away from Boston records and the families I was seeking information on. He suggested I contact Robert Mussey, a furniture conservator in the Boston area who did a great deal of research on Boston furniture of the late eighteenth century (one more expert witness). I found him with a quick Google search and was quickly overwhelmed by his credentials and scholarly publications. Deciding to investigate a bit more on my own before bothering him with my simple questions, I put Mr. Mussey's contact information in the case file for after the holidays and continued to dig for evidence.

this is emptying fast enough, indeed, indeed Miss Nancy, I hope y——
enough, I shall think them's the last on 'em. the——
but I'll bring in some the landing up there, I ma——
full from the libery besides these here ——
once you wash
more

THE SUN
REPUBLI——
THE BATTERY
Tuckerg & Royal
TRIBUN-E SUN
INTELLigen REPUBLIC
HARLEPE——
Star
GLOBE
EXPRESS
WASHINGT——
ALEXANDRIA GAZI——
CHRISTIAN REGISTER

FINAL SCENE 'IN THE Front Parlor at——

5

The Evidence

Part I: The Dawes Collection

How could I prove Richard Cranch once owned George's secretary? I needed facts; more importantly, I needed evidence. Unfortunately, I had run out of leads and out of ideas for where to find more.

I went back through my case file, looking for any clues I might have overlooked. I reread Brock Jobe's email, which suggested I scour the inside boards and drawers of George's secretary for any signs left behind by the original craftsman, or even Richard Cranch.

Had he written his signature somewhere, perhaps on one of the unfinished boards, as he was known to do?

This type of project would require removing the bookcase from the desk, something I could not do by myself. I decided to settle for a partial inspection instead. To my surprise, the bottom of the drawers were all numbered with what looked like graphite. Were these marks left by the cabinetmaker? Probably, but nothing remarkable enough to identify the person who had made them or why. I found no other notable marks.

I began to wonder if the other Dawes Collection items that George had given my mother might hold additional clues — or, better yet, answers — to this harassing mystery. So while visiting with her one day I asked her to pull out "everything George." She was more than eager to oblige. In fact, my mother started rummaging through her house like a gameshow contestant given the task of finding items hidden under every seat in the auditorium and I began to wonder if she would ever run out of hidden storage spots. Some things hung on a wall while others took up unnoticed space in a knickknack cabinet in her living room.

She started placing her finds on the kitchen table. Many pieces I recalled seeing as a child but I was also surprised to discover a number I had never seen before.

"This is everything," she finally announced, her kitchen table looking more like a display case at one of her favorite antique shops. "Except for the silverware," she added. Out came an enormous cardboard box filled with a variety of silverware, pieces of every kind, big and small. I am sure the sight of everything laid out together is what convinced her it was time for me to become the caretaker of the entire Dawes Collection, to include all of the items she had been holding back.

Within a few days, I was reuniting the remaining collection with its seasoned ancestor, George's secretary. And once home, sitting in my study with the complete collection laid out before me, my investigative juices began to flow uncontrollably. I could not wait to explore the history of each piece and, if possible, discover what had belonged to whom. I was back to the basics, Investigations 101, you might say. It was time to dig down deep into these items to see if they revealed any hidden clues or connections to Richard Cranch.

Diving into the Rabbit Hole. . .

As mentioned, a rabbit hole is information that usually leads an investigator to places they would not routinely go. Sometimes these places utterly surprise and amaze us by producing the investigation's most unimaginable evidence. Sometimes they produce, well…nothing, resulting in a colossal waste of time and resources. And agents never know which outcome will materialize until they go down into the hole and start exploring every twist and turn.

The last prosecutor I worked with was notorious for sending agents down into every imaginable rabbit hole. As I came across new and unexplored holes, I soon learned not to ask if I should explore them. Instead, I just jumped in, looked around, and then presented the prosecutor with my results before he even knew it existed.

In this case, each thing my mother dug out of the hidden places in her house, every item in the Dawes Collection, was an unexplored rabbit hole needing my full attention and investigative expertise. Perhaps one of them would reveal a connection to Richard Cranch and prove that he had once owned George's secretary. I would not know what was there until I jumped into all of the holes with both feet and poked around.

... And What I Found There

Here are some of the more interesting discoveries I made:

"Patent" pocket watch with gold hunter case, Dawes coat of arms engraved on outer-front casing, English hallmarks on inner-back casing, 22-inch gold-braided watch chain

The question at hand: who had been the owner of this beautiful gold pocket watch? Given the Dawes coat of arms engraved on the front cover, I took the liberty of assuming it had belonged to a Dawes family member.

As luck—and let it be known that this has been a critical element in more than one of my fraud investigations—would have it, while I was waiting to hear back from the Massachusetts Probate Office, I spent additional time researching Colonel

Dawes. I came across an interesting RootsWeb.com article about American silversmiths that highlighted a silver punch bowl made by William Holmes, engraved on one side with the Dawes coat of arms and given to the colonel by his field officers and captains of the regiment in 1763, to commemorate his service. The article cited a section from the colonel's will that had stated, "…to my Grandson Thomas Dawes Tertius after the decease of his Grandmother Dawes my Gold Watch and Silver Bowl.…"

This same punch bowl was donated in 1913 to the Museum of Fine Arts in Boston by Martha Dawes, widow of Ambrose Dawes (George's uncle). The *Museum of Fine Arts Bulletin*, reported this about the bowl in April 1913, "Ambrose Dawes, the last possessor of the bowl, was the great-grandson of the colonel, and had received it as a legacy from his cousin Rev. Thomas Dawes of Brewster, Mass. who had used it as a baptismal basin."

At the time of his death, the Reverend Thomas Dawes, son of Thomas Dawes Tertius, was a widower with no children. To keep the colonel's legacy intact, he had but two living male first cousins to pass the keepsakes to: John Greenleaf Dawes, the son of Harrison and Lucy Dawes, and Ambrose Dawes, the son of George and Mary Dawes. Having moved to California permanently sometime around 1850, John was considered a pioneer. Ambrose lived in Boston and probably maintained close contact with Thomas over the years. In my mind, the choice was simple and supported by the *Museum of Fine Arts Bulletin*.

Logic told me the gold watch had followed the same path. However, as much as it might seem logical, I needed to answer two particularly important questions. Had the Reverend received the Colonel's gold watch from his father (Thomas Tertius) and, if so, had he passed it on to Ambrose? If the answer to both questions was yes, then Martha (Ambrose's wife), after donating the punch bowl to the museum, had most likely sent the gold watch to Ambrose's nephew George in San Francisco. George and his brother Rufus were two of the last surviving male members of the Colonel's line. The responsibility of continuing the Colonel's legacy and family name now fell to them, though, sadly, neither one was able to fulfil it.

My theory seemed flawless but what could I actually prove? Unfortunately, like everything else in the collection, George never mentioned the story behind the watch or its previous owners. Also, the timeline for the watch made me realize something else: not everything in the Dawes Collection had arrived in the shipment of goods the family sent to Richard in San Francisco sometime in the 1890s.

No matter who had once owned the watch, its engraved case was an intriguing piece of art. I could not help myself from doing a bit more research. Inside the back casing were what appeared to be three English hallmarks, an indication the casing was English made. I found a website on the history and order of English hallmarks. I tried but had difficulty making sense of the marks I found on my piece. According to the site's reference guides, a lion mark indicated the piece was made of sterling silver. My piece was gold. Another mark should have indicated the approximate time-period when the case was made. I could not find anything similar to this mark in the guide, so I emailed the chap behind the website and attached a picture of the hallmarks to see if he could shed any light.

His response led to a new kind of bizarre and unbelievable incident—the kind that makes you laugh: The hallmarks on the watch case were "pseudo hallmarks." During the eighteenth century, when England was the best and preferred watch manufacturer for the time, watches were made in Switzerland, brought to America, and stamped with pseudo hallmarks to give unsuspecting buyers the impression they were English made. My watch, or (possibly) the Colonel's, was a fraud. Beautifully engraved but designed to fool buyers into paying more than it was worth. (Too bad the statute of limitations expired centuries earlier. I would have opened another case.)

American Waltham pocket watch, tricolor (silver, gold, and copper) with hunter case and 22-inch gold watch chain

Using the serial number found stamped inside this watch, I queried the Pocket Watch Database (yes, there is such a thing) to learn the piece was American made, manufactured in Waltham, Massachusetts, between 1895 and '98. There was no indication who in the family might have owned it. Richard Cranch Dawes (George's father) was still alive when the watch was made, as were his brothers Ambrose and George who both lived in Boston (near Waltham) at that time.

But there was another possibility: Within the Dawes Collection, I found a picture of George and Rufus as young boys. Rufus was still wearing knickers and could not have been much more than ten or eleven years old, making George thirteen or fourteen in his suit with a coat vest. Laced through one of the vest buttonholes was a gold watch chain. George had turned thirteen in 1897, well within the production range of this American Waltham watch. It could have been his first watch.

I also discovered a picture of Ambrose Dawes in an article about his life in the Memorial Encyclopedia of the State of Massachusetts (Vol. 2, pages 220–3, 1918). I examined Ambrose's face looking for features resembling George. Finding none, I was instead rewarded by another detail. There, openly displayed and hanging from his coat vest, a double Albert T-bar pocket watch chain. There is no way of knowing which watch is hiding inside Ambrose's vest pocket—the gold watch engraved with the Dawes coat of arms, the American Waltham, or possibly another.

Though interesting items, neither provided me with a connection to Richard Cranch.

Rufus and George, ages 10 and 13

Oil painting of a young boy (student) – Painted on wood, measuring 7.5" x 9.5"

This was the oil painting I sent to AuctionWatch.com for an evaluation. (You will see more details on this item later in this chapter.)

Wooden nocturnal pointer – Date and origin unknown

This item took some time to identify even though it was clearly labeled on the handle as a "Nocturnal Pointer," which it turns out was once used to determine local time at night based on the position of two or more stars. Richard Cranch Dawes served in the US Navy, so I assign the item to him, though my assumption is unsubstantiated.

Young girl's stitch sampler – Circa 1840

The words embroidered into the fabric tell us this stitch sampler was sewn by "Mary E. Dawes, Aged 11 Years, 1840." Stitch samplers were a common tool girls used to learn and develop basic needlework skills. I now knew this was Nanty's work.

Old wooden box, original pull handle and front-locking device intact, original hinges replaced

Based on its construction and the remaining original hardware, I believe this box was crafted pre-1800s. While reviewing Richard Cranch's probate inventory I came across an item described as a "tea chest." Tea was a pricy commodity in Cranch's day, often stored in a tea caddy that normally came with a lock. I found myself wondering if this might be that tea chest but it's another dead end. I have no way of knowing its true purpose or whether it is connected to Cranch. For now, it will continue to serve the purpose my mother gave it: storing smaller personal items from the Dawes Collection.

When I first opened this box, I felt like I was in the middle of a search warrant having just discovered a file cabinet full of cash and key financial documents. Inside the box were more collectibles containing clues and possibly evidence connecting Dawes family members to one another. I discovered the old family photograph of George and Rufus here and another of George when he was about three years old. There was a photograph of an unidentified young girl (no more than three years old) mounted in a small wooden oval frame. But I was more interested in a photo of George's father, who, as a young man in his thirties, lacked any resemblance to George whatsoever. However, that evaluation changed when I placed Richard's photo next to the one of George as a teenager. The family resemblance is definitely there.

Inside a separate envelope, I found the original obituary clippings from local Quincy newspapers for Richard's parents, George Minot Dawes (1802–1871) and Mary Elizabeth (Greenleaf) Dawes (1806–1886) and Richard's brother George Greenleaf Dawes (1832–1899). There was also a set of gold cuff links engraved with the initials "GGD," obviously belonging to George Greenleaf Dawes.

The last item was a small handwritten note inside a matching envelope, addressed to George Minot Dawes. The note, penned by his Uncle George Greenleaf Dawes but written for Mary E. Dawes, was dated January 1, 1885. I believe it had accompanied the ornate silver birthday cup she sent to honor his birth. As much as I had always admired the silver cup, I had never seen this personal note before which read, in part:

Dear Georgie,
Your Grandma sends you a New Years card. She would
write to you but she is not quite well enough. She hopes
the warmth of your grandpa whose name you have will
descend upon time and bless you with love.

Family silverware collection — a gazillion pieces

I grew up with the Dawes family silverware never realizing how
many pieces were in the collection. I was always intrigued by the
fancy initials engraved at the tip of the long handles of their
oversized silver serving spoons, which were always used at
every major holiday dinner: Christmas, Easter, Thanksgiving, my
father's birthday — and George's. These were the holidays George
celebrated with us. I found it curious that some of the handles
were engraved with the initial "G" and others with a combination of initials. I remember asking myself, "If these are from
George's family, why isn't the letter "D" engraved on any of the
handles?" Then someone would pass the mashed potatoes and
my question was forgotten until the next holiday dinner.

This time, reexamining one of those spoons produced
another OSOD ("Oh shit, oh dear!") discovery. Those beautifully
engraved, multi-letter inscriptions on some of the spoons spelled
out "JLG." In other words, we served our mashed potatoes and
green beans with spoons that had belonged to George's great-
grandparents John and Lucy Greenleaf, probably crafted around
1795, the year of their marriage. Over two hundred years of
exceptional care had kept them in pristine condition. I could not
believe our family unknowingly celebrated each holiday using
Greenleaf family serving spoons. More importantly, I now had

hard evidence that items from the Greenleaf family were passed down to George. Richard Cranch was only one generation away.

I decided the contents of the silverware box deserved a full inventory. Could there be other spectacular finds among these forks and spoons? I laid out each piece and then matched it to others in the collection by size, style, pattern, and engravings. I found another set of large serving spoons made by a different craftsman. Only one initial, the letter "G," appeared on the handles, indicating ownership by a Greenleaf. These pieces appeared to be much older. Perhaps John and Lucy had also owned these, or John's parents, William and Mary (Brown) Greenleaf.

Another unsolved mystery with no answer.

The Cranch Connection

I continued my silverware inventory, unprepared for the next big discovery: I matched up five small teaspoons displaying a similar pattern and style as the large serving spoons with the "JLG" inscription. I honestly expected to see the same initials on the handles, connecting them to the set. However, the engraved initials appearing on these spoons read "RMC," meaning only one thing: these spoons had belonged to Richard and Mary (Smith) Cranch (George's great-great-grandparents) and may have been in the mouth of First Lady Abigail Adams—and maybe even a President of the United States (John Adams) at some point! Mary and her sister Abigail had lived within a half mile of each other in Quincy. I could imagine them sitting in the parlor of the Cranch House, sipping tea together on a chilly winter afternoon, these spoons resting on cup saucers.

Incredibly, I had experienced two OSOD discoveries in one day, both of which naturally required exuberant happy dances around my study. Finding the Cranch and Greenleaf spoons was like finding a treasure chest with gold and silver coins inside. I held a piece of history between my fingers, the missing link to the line of descent for a family item, all the way from Richard Cranch to his great-great-grandson George Dawes. The same line I was trying to prove about George's secretary.

So far, the silver inventory had been the most productive and rewarding rabbit hole in the collection. The hours I had spent jumping into and exploring the unknown were well justified.

These types of rewards keep fraud investigators motivated and engaged with their work, especially when logical leads dry up and the case continues to linger on for what can seem like an eternity, much like this investigation. I now had a connection to Richard Cranch but it still was not enough.

Regrettably, unexpected family issues required my immediate and full-time attention, so I restocked the cold storage unit and closed the door again, this time for another eight months.

Antiques Roadshow **Wanna-be**

By January 2010, I was ready to jump back into my investigation and I happened to notice an advertisement in the newspaper for an upcoming antique workshop sponsored by a local auction house. It was one of those "bring in an item or two" *Antiques Roadshow*-type gatherings. I mentioned it to my mother, thinking it might be fun to take a couple Dawes Collection items in for an evaluation and she agreed.

I chose to take the oil painting, something we had never followed up on and still knew little about. I was also curious about George's silver birthday cup. I met with Josh Levine, the owner of the auction house, who seemed eager to examine my two items. He found the silver cup "delightful" but not worth much. His reaction to the painting was more exciting.

Given its size, and the fact it was painted on wood, he believed the painting to be quite old, probably eighteenth century. Since it had no signature to identify the artist, he asked if I could leave the painting with him so he could confer with one of his colleagues. I was thrilled to see someone taking an interest in the painting, and I took the opportunity to mention George's secretary and inquire about an updated appraisal. Josh was intrigued and offered to come to my home to take a closer look.

About a week later, Josh arrived and took pictures of George's secretary from every angle and I shared everything I knew about its connection to the Dawes, Greenleaf, and Cranch families. He wanted to consult further with another colleague, particularly a person who specialized in eighteenth-century pieces who felt George's secretary had been crafted as early as 1750 to '55 (the third such opinion by an expert).

My meeting with Josh also prompted a discussion about the future of George's secretary. By this time, the Watts family had served faithfully as caretaker of the piece for over fifty-five years. When you refer to an item in your home as "George's secretary" for all of those years, it never really feels like it belongs to you. In my heart I believed it needed a forever home closer to its place of origin where it could be admired for the history it represented and had witnessed. I hoped for an old historic home in New England or a museum. Josh suggested putting it up for auction, which was cause for a family discussion.

In the meantime, Josh returned the oil painting. His associates confirmed it was eighteenth century, most likely around 1780. Surprisingly, they were able to establish a European origin (rather than American, as AuctionWatch.com had stated), maybe Amsterdam or nearby. The artist remained a mystery.

My head spun. The items in the Dawes Collection had one strong common denominator between them: they were all somehow connected to a member of George's extended family or their family history. I suspected the family would not keep such a painting, a portrait, of just any young lad for over one hundred years if he was not a family member. Who could he be?

Time for a New Timeline

With my investigator cap in place, I began asking the basic questions to map out a new timeline. Who in the family was a young boy around 1780? Richard and Mary's son William was born in 1769, making him about the right age, but I found no record or report of William ever traveling abroad as a youngster.

Who in the family had travelled abroad during those years? Mary's brother-in-law, then-Secretary of State John Adams and his two young sons. John Quincy was a teenager at the time; however, his younger brother Charles would have been ten or eleven. The boys studied in Amsterdam and Leiden. A pastel portrait of John Quincy Adams hangs in the National Portrait Gallery in Washington, DC, drawn by Isaak Schmidt who had founded an art academy in Amsterdam. I wondered if anyone had painted Charles while they were there? An unknown student perhaps? I had far more questions than answers.

I decided to reach out to the experts on the Adams family and sent a general inquiry to the curator at the Adams National Historical Park in Quincy, Massachusetts, explaining my connection to the Cranch family and the painting I discovered within the

Dawes Collection. The curator found my theory intriguing but her research shed no light on the matter.

To satisfy my own curiosity, I decided to do a deeper dive into the Adams diaries available online through the Massachusetts Historical Society, hoping to find mention of Charles sitting for a portrait while he was overseas. While it was worth my time, if only to be able to check off this one box for remote possibilities, the identity of this young lad remains unknown, a frustrating reminder that not every mystery can be solved.

To my surprise, the Adams National Historical Park curator asked if she could share my contact information with an associate who was currently researching Richard and Mary Cranch. Checking my email a few days later I was confused to see the name "Robert Mussey" in my inbox. The name rang a bell: it was the gentleman Brock Jobe had referred me to two years earlier and who I never reached out to. At first, I thought someone was forwarding me an article he had written but the message was from Mr. Mussey himself, the curator's associate. Who would believe the target of my investigation, dead for two hundred years, provided the perfect introduction to this expert witness? (Another bizarre and unbelievable incident to add to the pile.)

Robert explained that he was working on a biography of the family of Richard and Mary Cranch. I was thrilled but a bit overwhelmed. His experience researching historic documents was more than I could ever hope or want to have. I was but a mere novice trying to prove a theory, he was the expert researcher.

I cannot emphasis enough how important it is to have someone like Robert on your investigative team, especially when the matter under investigation falls outside your own experience and abilities. Meeting and working with these kinds of individuals transforms a routine investigation into something extraordinary.

During the last ten years of my investigation, Robert shared his own research findings with me but, more importantly, he encouraged and advised me on what to do whenever I hit the infamous brick wall.

About this time, I reached out to Renee to see if she was any closer to taking on Nanty's letters. Though her life was still too full of other commitments, she told me that the Great Northwest Bookstore, where she had originally purchased the letters, had recently burned to the ground. I marvel at how close we came to losing Nanty's legacy. Chances are, had Renee not purchased the letters when she did, they would have been part of the blaze; mere ashes, lost forever.

Another Dawes Collectible

By the summer of 2010, after a number of lengthy discussions, my family agreed it was time to find George's secretary and some pieces from the Dawes Collection a new home. I contacted Josh to start the process. For several reasons, he wanted to wait until the first of the next year, when he held a special yearly auction.

Being in no hurry, I turned my attention back to the collection, as there was still more research to do. By this time, I thought I had collected "everything George" but I was wrong.

After my mother had shared the news about the auction with her cousin Marilyn in Washington state, she informed me that Marilyn was moving into an assisted living facility and wanted to know if I would like the silver piece she had given her.

"What silver piece?" I asked.

"One that belonged to George. She always liked it so I gave it to her about thirty years ago. It looked like a saltshaker or something similar."

When the small box arrived in the mail I immediately opened it and pushed the wrapping paper aside. Even though the item was not related to the Cranch and Greenleaf families, this charming, beautifully handcrafted little silver piece had some interesting initials engraved on the side, "D T*H.": Dawes, Thomas and Hannah, who had married in 1752.

I was holding a "caster," used to sprinkle spices on food, that had once belonged to Colonel Dawes and his wife. Marilyn was delighted when I told her the significance of what had been sitting in her China closet all those years and to know her special piece was to be reunited with the rest of the collection.

As the day of the auction grew closer, I was plagued by second thoughts, wondering if selling the collection was the right thing to do. I wondered if George would approve of what we were doing and worried the items would not be properly cared for. You would have thought these pieces were my children and I was finding foster homes for each one. Which, in a sense, I was.

The worst was when Josh's company picked up George's secretary from my home and transported it to the auction house. The spot where it once sat was now strangely empty. I cried all afternoon. I am sure it was a case of separation anxiety.

The Endless Roller Coaster Ride

To be a buyer at an auction is fun and exciting; to be the seller is pure hell. It is the *Antiques Roadshow* on steroids and other mind-blowing drugs. Our items were being sold separately by category, so over and over I sat patiently through the nerve-racking ritual of hearing about each piece and then waiting breathlessly for that first bid.

Opening bids offend. You wait for the next. Let me rephrase that, you hope for the next. If it comes, the sound of that higher amount excites something deep inside. I have never had an addiction. However, I now understand what it is like to suffer from one. The sound of each growing bid became my "fix" and I could not wait for the next. By the time the final offer was accepted, I wondered if my heartbeat would ever return to a normal rhythm.

The auction lasted for three painful hours, offering everything from art to silver to jewelry to furniture. With such a variety of items, each adrenaline-induced roller coaster ride barely ended before it was time to board another car. I could have thrown up at any moment from the stress of each sale. The books and silver went quickly, the gold watch went to a person with the last name of Dawes (I have no idea from which line).

As the third hour approached, it was finally time for George's secretary to be offered up. Josh had advertised nationwide, allowing for online and telephone bids. As the bidding started, I could feel my heart jumping out of my chest once again. First one offer, then another. The numbers were slowly escalating, as was my blood pressure. When that final bid came in, I am not sure if I was relieved or disappointed.

In an auction, not every item brings in the top dollar you hope for. This is why I met with Josh beforehand and placed a "reserve" price on George's secretary, the oil painting, and the drawing by C.P. Cranch. The final bid on the secretary was just a few thousand dollars short of my reserve, so I was not obligated to sell it. The item that had driven this entire process was still with me, while other items of the collection were gone. For some reason, I felt bad about the collection being separated. George's secretary would be returning home along with the oil painting and drawing.

I was happy to learn that Robert Mussey purchased the set of "RMC" teaspoons (I kept one for my own collection). Who better to have them? I sent him the drawing of the Cranch Greenleaf House, to be used as a motivator for his book with the understanding it would be donated to the Massachusetts Historical Society once his research was completed. (Not only did he later take care of the donation but he included the set of spoons along with it.)

The roller coaster ride from hell left me physically, mentally, and emotionally drained. George's secretary was restored to its place of honor in my home, its family history (and mystery) continuing to lay claim to my free time, just not so intensely.

A few months later, in Boston for a few days, I finally had the opportunity to meet Robert Mussey. What better place for introductions than at the John Adams National Historic Park. After Robert had taken me on an amazing tour, I escorted him to Hancock Cemetery, a place he had never visited, and introduced him to George's family. Richard and Mary Cranch are also interred there. In his book, *The Adams Women*, Paul Nagel writes, "the venerable partners [Richard & Mary Cranch] were laid side by side in the Adams tomb; they had no cemetery plot of their own, their estate being comprised mostly of debt."

Taking a Break in Afghanistan

By October, proving Richard Cranch once owned George's secretary felt like an impossible task. I had reached and confronted the brick wall with little success. I was ready for a new challenge in my life. An old associate of mine had retired months earlier and gone to work for the Special Inspector General for Afghanistan Reconstruction (SIGAR). She called me from Kabul, Afghanistan, to ask if I would be interested in coming back to work and keeping her company in an otherwise all-male unit. At first I laughed hysterically at the idea, but soon realized it was an offer of a lifetime. I could not wait to sign on, and after a year in Afghanistan, I transferred to SIGAR's headquarters in Arlington, Virginia, where I stayed for another three.

Naturally, the Cranch investigation sat in the cold storage locker during this entire time. However, shortly after I settled into my new townhouse in Alexandria, Virginia, I reached out to Robert Mussey to update him about my new location. We continued to share snippets of information pertaining to the Cranch, Greenleaf, and Dawes families as they surfaced but after fourteen years of investigating I had to concede I had not met the burden of proof to positively say Richard Cranch had once owned George's secretary.

"We lack the clincher," Robert said, describing two possible scenarios in his mind.

1. His first hope was the same as Brock Job's years earlier: finding an inscription somewhere on the secretary that would link it to the Cranch family. Neither my amateur review nor the thorough inspection conducted by Josh Levine and his associates prior to the auction had turned anything up.

2. His second hope was that we would yet discover a historic letter or other document that mentioned or described the desk. Even he acknowledged how extremely unlikely it would be to find such a document outside the hands of family members. I had a lingering hope for Nanty's letters

but unfortunately, Renee was no closer to working on her project and I did not have any time to offer either.

For the first time since I had initiated this investigation, I was to the point of believing the mystery would remain unsolved forever.

Given Robert's vast research on Cranch, he shared his own theory about the secretary with me: The Cranches were not wealthy people. They may have purchased the piece from relatives, acquaintances, or at public auction. So, George's secretary could have been a piece of used furniture—meaning Richard Cranch was likely "an" owner rather than the original owner.

This did make perfect sense. Our furniture experts all agreed George's secretary was crafted between 1750 and '55. And Richard Cranch had arrived in America from England in 1746 at age twenty, initially making his living as a watchmaker and not marrying until 1762. On a practical note, knowing firsthand how difficult it is to move the mahogany monstrosity, I wondered what bachelor would want to buy and lug around such an item before he had a permanent home to settle into. As Brock Jobe said, it was an item suitable for one's parlor. So the question now became when did Richard and Mary start purchasing household furniture, given their limited resources? Thinking about a timeline again, and if Cranch was not the original owner, I wondered if the piece could have been sitting in the Virchild House when Cranch rented it.

The Expert Witness Evaluation

In 2016, Robert contacted me to ask if a good friend of his, the leading expert on Boston and Charlestown furniture of this period, who had just retired as a professor at the University of

Delaware, could examine George's secretary. Before Robert even spoke his friend's name those clues told me he was describing one of my other expert witnesses: Brock Jobe. Talk about full circle! (And another bizarre and unbelievable incident to add to the ever-growing list.)

I seriously doubt Brock recalled exchanging emails with me thirteen years earlier about the same piece but a few months later he came to my townhouse and spent four to five hours examining every drawer and surface of George's secretary.

While his findings surprised me, when I reread my mother's emails from 2000, the full story fell together without any conflicting issues and gave me answers to several long-standing questions.

In Brock's review, he reported the piece was consistent with eighteenth-century Boston construction but he had not been able to identify a craftsman. He was quite impressed with the late-nineteenth-century repairs stating, "Whoever renovated this desk and bookcase in the late [nineteenth] century was a highly skilled craftsman. The caliber of the new work is as good, if not better, than the original workmanship." He did not believe the desktop lid was original, however, the restorer had chosen a dense, heavy piece of mahogany, a very fine wood.

The restoration work had been more extensive than my family was aware of. Brock, first under the impression the repairs had been done in Boston by one of two companies in the area at that time, was set straight by my mother's email, which stated that George's secretary "was damaged at the time it was brought to California. Restoration work was done (in San Francisco) at the end of the 1800s—both workman and materials were of the best available. The wood was matched from the woods out of the

Boston area." This explained Brock's assumptions about the repairs.

Unfortunately, even with his own thorough review, Brock was not able to find any markings that could be contributed to Richard Cranch, leaving me to wonder if there ever was such a mark or signature. Perhaps there had been, on one of the inner pieces of wood, replaced over a hundred years earlier. Yet another unanswered question.

With these thorough inspections conducted by both Josh and Brock, I had to cross off item one from Robert's clincher list and conclude that the piece had no identifying marks anywhere.

However, that still left Robert's second item, the impossible-to-find family letters and documents. Was there evidence like this that would prove my case? If so, the discovery would have to wait. George's secretary and I were moving back to the Arizona desert where my work with SIGAR would continue on a part-time basis from my home office.

My only imaginable way forward, if one existed, still laid with Nanty's letters.

...elest Miss Nanty, I hope you don't think
...'s the last on 'em, there's three more on
...landing up there, & one in the pralges room,
...is there here —

Sarah you hav'nt em up-
in & I'le smak em up-
here's one for husband
the girl

Why don't y-
put in thes-
one of Maggie
pin a nest
in looks a-
must be the
of a sma-
in the ea-
the day

Front Parlor at "Grandc Hall"

6

The Intent

Fraud investigations are all about paper trails and finding key evidence buried somewhere within a pile of innocent-looking documents that prove a defendant defrauded the US government out of thousands of dollars or more. Without these original and authentic documents, an agent would not have a case. However, in a court of law, finding and presenting this evidence is only the first step to securing a conviction. Another critical element must be proven: we must show the defendant intended to defraud the government.

Proving Intent

Take a look at Title 18 of the United States Code, Section 1031 — Major fraud against the United States (italics mine): "Whoever, knowingly executes, or attempts to execute, any scheme or artifice *with the intent* — (1) to defraud the United States; or (2) to obtain money or property by means of false or fraudulent pretenses...."

The key word here is "intent." To eliminate any possibility of a defendant claiming their actions were a simple mistake or misunderstanding, the evidence must show both how they executed the scheme and their state of mind when they committed the fraud. This is no easy task. What seems obvious to the investigator who knows the case inside and out may not be to a jury.

How does a Special Agent prove intent? We look for correspondence (such as letters, emails, text messages) written by the defendant telling someone what he or she was planning to do and why. Or we find witnesses that overheard or saw the defendant purposely do something to further a fraudulent act.

Getting to Know George Dawes

As I have said before, this is not a criminal matter: I am just trying to connect a man from long ago to a piece of furniture that now sits in my house. So intent doesn't apply to this investigation in the standard sense. However, I do believe the question of intent should be asked of George Dawes, my mother's beloved friend.

George entrusted my mother with all of his family's historic and personal treasures — but did he intend to leave her in the dark about the provenance associated with each historic family piece or did he himself not know the details of their origin? Recall my mother's words about George in one of her emails, "In the time I knew him I never got to where I could ask him anything about his personal life. It would only come out in bits and parts...."

I find it hard to believe that someone with personal connections back to Abigail Adams and Colonel Thomas Dawes would not be more forthcoming about their ancestry. And as the caretaker of his family's remaining treasures, I would think he would be fully aware of each item, some dating back to as early as 1752. However, if he did not know their rich histories, I am left wondering why not.

Trying to answer this question helped me realize just how little I really knew about George. I had spent years investigating the members of his family, to the point I now knew more about these people than George ever did. It was time to turn my attention and investigative skills toward George and complete his own subject sheet. I knew the basics:

- *Birth:* San Francisco, California, 20 November 1884
- *Parents:* Richard Cranch and Emma (Kline/ Anderson) Dawes
- *Marriage:* Mary (Strong) Griffin in or about 1925; no issue
- *Work:* Accountant/auditor
- *Residence:* Lived his entire life in the San Francisco area until he retired and then relocated to Sacramento
- *Death:* 6 November 1972, age eighty-seven, due to complications of a stroke
- *Resting place:* The Masonic Lawn Cemetery in Sacramento, California

George Dawes, at age 3 and 82

I also had my own recollections about George (keeping in mind my memories are those of a young girl). I remember him as this little old man (he was already seventy-two when I was born), hunched over a bit, with thinning greyish hair (blond at one time) combed over to the side. His blue eyes would sparkle behind the wire-rimmed glasses that rested on his big nose (a Dawes feature). He was a quiet, reserved person with a soft laugh, more of a giggle really, his way of hiding his yellowed teeth which were all original but stained from age and the lack of proper dental care over the years. George always carried small pieces of paper and a pencil in his shirt pocket, readily available for recording notes on expenditures or other information he wanted to retain or give to my mother. And he always wore khaki pants that were about one or two sizes too big for him, cinched at the waist with a brown leather belt. Plus a black bolo tie, his signature piece.

I never addressed him as George; he was always "Mr. Dawes" to me. But whenever he visited, we had fun together. He always had a dollar bill ready for me in his pocket. He was always willing to help in any way he could. I once needed a full-length picture of someone to complete a requirement for my Girl Scout photography badge. He graciously volunteered. Each Christmas, I would receive one special gift from Mr. Dawes. It was always something that surpassed anything my parents would have bought me. I guess I was the one little girl in his life he felt he could spend money on. In my freshman year of high school, he gave me a stereo which traveled with me to college.

The last time I saw George he was in a nursing home—a horrible place to be back in those days—after his stroke. The once proud but modest little man stood in a hospital gown, feet bare, not knowing where he was or who was visiting him. He mumbled uncontrollably during our short visit. It broke my heart to see him that way. I could not bear the thought of returning for a second visit. I did not have to; he died shortly after.

As young people do, I rarely thought of George during the first few months after he passed. Until one morning in my

American History class at school. My teacher believed in the power of movies and showed us historic productions several times a week. This particular day we were watching a film about vice presidents of the United States. About halfway through, the vice president under Calvin Coolidge came onscreen, full of life and stirring every emotion inside my body. With tears running down my cheeks, I felt like I was seeing George — or someone who could have passed for his twin brother. It was in fact Vice President Charles Gates Dawes, a direct descendant of William Who Rode, and a not-so-distant cousin to George. The resemblance was uncanny, right down to his blondish grey hair and big Dawes nose.

Returning home later, I felt drawn to George's secretary. I opened the bookcase and pulled out one of the books stored inside, this one quite new compared to the others and one I had never taken an interest in until that very moment: *Portrait of an American* by Bascom Timmons, published in 1953, was all about the life of Charles Gates Dawes. I stared at the portrait inside the front cover for a long time, amazed once again by the family resemblance. Inside the book I found a letter, addressed to George and postmarked November 21, 1924. The return address read, "Charles G. Dawes, Evanston, Illinois." It was a personal letter to George from his famous cousin who wrote, "My dear Mr. Dawes: I have your telegram of November 6, and thank you for your congratulations. Yours, Charles G. Dawes (signature)." I was touching a piece of American history, one that was not in a museum or antique shop. Nothing in my history class had ever touched me so deeply.

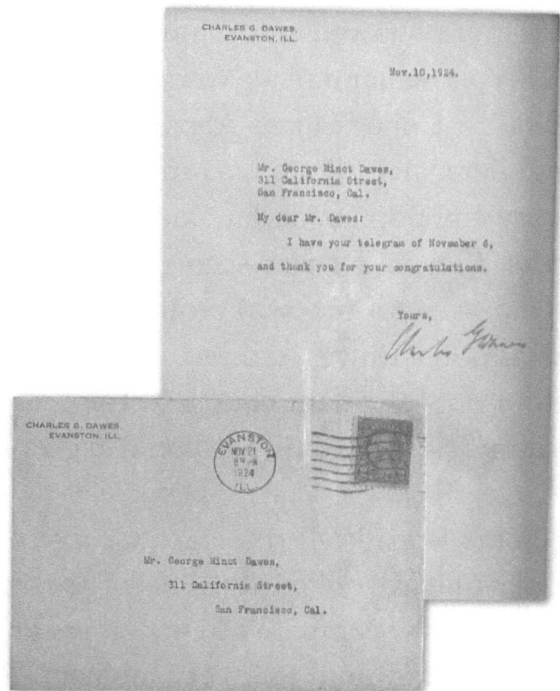

At some point before he died, George told my mother to place any remaining funds from his estate into a college fund for me. It was his last special gift — or so I thought. When I graduated from college a few years later, my mother presented me with a small box from "Mr. Dawes." Inside was a gold chain necklace, which my mother had someone make from one of the Dawes Collection's three gold pocket watch chains and gave to me as a remembrance of George's contribution to my education. Except for the year I spent in Afghanistan, that chain has been around my neck ever since.

These were all very personal memories that added nothing to understanding George's upbringing or his relationships with his family. It was time to dig deeper and fill in all the blank boxes on George's background form.

George's Father, Richard Cranch Dawes

Richard Cranch Dawes was already forty-six years old when George was born. I often wonder if Richard was a man of words or more like George, soft spoken and secretive. Family history is usually handed down from one generation to the next, and it would have been up to Richard to bridge the information gap between the family he left behind in Massachusetts and the sons he was raising three thousand miles away in San Francisco. But was he successful in doing so?

Richard was born and raised in the Cranch Greenleaf House in Quincy, with his sister Mary (Nanty), older brother George, and younger brother Ambrose. As we know, the family moved out of their long-time home around 1856 or '57. The 1860 US Census places Richard with his family in Melrose, a few miles away from Quincy. He enlisted in the Union Army in 1862, during the Civil War. After being discharged in 1863, he enlisted in the Navy (corroborating my mother's understanding) where he stayed until January 1867. Richard mustered out in San Francisco, possibly deciding then to make this city his permanent residence, though no one knows why he decided to leave his Boston roots and relocate so far away from his family.

Richard's name appeared in the 1868 *San Francisco City Directory* as a resident living with John G. Dawes, his cousin and the son of Harrison and Lucy (Greenleaf) Dawes. John was an early pioneer, arriving in San Francisco sometime before 1861, and then relocating to Fresno around 1870.

Richard married Charlotte Ann Howe, his second cousin from Haverhill, Massachusetts, in October 1870. His sister, Mary "Nanty" (Dawes) Mitchell, died in January 1870 and, given the completion of the Pacific Railroad in 1869 that now connected the west coast with the east, I wondered if he returned to Boston for a brief visit after her death and met up with Charlotte during this time. In any case, at some point Charlotte had traveled to San Francisco and the two were married there. Their daughter, Mary Nantie Dawes, obviously named after Richard's mother (Mary) and sister (Nanty), was born in October 1871. Sadly, Richard suffered the loss of several family members over the next ten years, including his father, George Minot Dawes in 1871, his daughter Mary Nantie in 1874, his Aunt Lucy in 1877, and his wife Charlotte in 1880.

Richard married Emma R. Kline/Anderson, a local woman from San Rafael, California who was twenty-two years his junior, in February 1884. Their son George Minot Dawes was born nine months later. A second son, Rufus, was born in March 1887.

Unfortunately, another string of family deaths occurred starting with his cousin Lucy Cranch "Bones" Dawes in 1884, his mother Mary E. (Greenleaf) Dawes in 1886, and his uncle Richard Cranch Greenleaf in 1887.

From 1884 to '88, Richard and Emma rented apartments in various buildings in San Francisco. Finally, in 1888, Richard was able to buy a home for the family at 1813 Eddy Street. According to the 1900 US Census, the home had no outstanding mortgage.

As a financial investigator, I found myself wondering how Richard was able to afford such a purchase. He was employed as a bookkeeper for Selby Smelting and Lead Company located at First and Howard Street for over twenty-five years. I could not find information indicating what his salary might have been in those days but a person's financial status does not depend solely on their salary. Family wills and probate records can provide amazing information, especially when those family members are located in Massachusetts.

As mentioned, probate records for Richard's mother indicated she left each son $1,583 ($42,725 in today's currency). Three years later Richard's uncle, Richard Greenleaf, an extremely wealthy man who made his money as a successful Boston merchant, left his nephew a sizable financial gift of $5,000 ($140,000 in today's currency). These funds would have been available to Richard just before he purchased his house.

I would normally search for evidence of such a purchase in documents stored within the city or county government offices. Unfortunately, the 1906 earthquake that destroyed much of San Francisco demolished City Hall and the property, birth, marriage, and death records created during the late nineteenth and early twentieth century that had been housed inside. So it was nearly impossible to check San Francisco city property records. Multiple condominium units now sit where the Dawes family home once was. Although current property values have skyrocketed in the San Francisco area, in 1888 the city was still developing and Richard would have had more than enough money at the time to pay for his house.

The fact that Richard owned a home in 1888 added weight to another one of my theories: I believe this may have been the year the bulk of the Dawes Collection—including the secretary—was shipped from Boston to San Francisco. Richard's older brother, George Greenleaf Dawes, lived with their parents in their Brookline home. City directories place George, an unmarried person, living with his cousin Harrison Dawes in Malden by 1888. GGD would have been left with the responsibility of closing down his parents' home after his mother's death in 1886 and dividing their assets between he and his two surviving brothers. Our George would have been four or five years old, which fits in with the memory he had shared with my mother about going to the docks as a youngster with his father to pick up a large shipment of family furniture and keepsakes.

Life in San Francisco for Richard and his family was quite comfortable and enjoyable during this era. Would a man like Richard, now at least fifty years of age, be discussing his lengthy line of dead relatives with his toddler son? I doubt it. Nor would this youngster have any interest in knowing about the origins of old family furniture, like the secretary that probably sat in the parlor of their home. Sadly, on December 2, 1898, when George was just fourteen, Richard Cranch Dawes died unexpectedly.

An interesting but sorrowful side note about Richard's burial: In December 1898, Richard was buried in the Odd Fellows Cemetery in San Francisco. However, in 1930, when the city decided to move all cemeteries (and the souls buried within them) outside the city limits, his remains were relocated to Greenlawn Memorial Park in San Mateo County. I found no paperwork on file regarding his reinternment, indicating he was most likely buried in a mass grave for unclaimed bodies. These are the souls whose families could not be located and notified at the time of removal and reinternment. Richard's daughter, Mary Nantie, was also among them leaving me to hope that she and Richard are together.

Richard left his family a sizable trust fund valued at $9,000 ($280,000 in today's currency). Half went to Emma, the other half was for his sons when they reached the age of maturity. And when Richard's brother, George Greenleaf Dawes, died the following year, he left George and Rufus another $12,000 ($370,000 in today's currency) to be added to their trust fund. The two boys were financially secure before age fifteen.

I started finding it easier to believe that George may not have known much about his family genealogy after all. With only his

Uncle Ambrose still alive but living in Boston, how would he? I seriously doubted George's mother could provide him with the details. Chances are she never met anyone from Richard's family. Other than making sure her boys stayed in touch with their Uncle Ambrose, there was little else she could provide.

George reached the age of maturity in 1905. According to a notice published in the *San Francisco Recorder* (a local newspaper) a hearing for the final accounting by George's guardian of trust took place in March 1906. The article indicated he was still living with Emma and Rufus at the family home on Eddy Street.

And if George's world had not been rocked enough by the early loss of his father, then events just a few weeks later on the morning of April 18, 1906, changed the course of his life forever: at 5:12 a.m. an earthquake measuring 7.9 on the Richter Scale hit the city of San Francisco, killing more than 3,000 people and displacing more than 250,000 residents (including George, his brother Rufus, and mother Emma). The quake destroyed 80 percent of the city, which at the time was home to 400,000 people.

I have no idea what this destruction did to the Dawes family home on Eddy Street, though, fortunately, the gas line fires did not reach George's neighborhood, I found a picture of Pierce Rudolph Storage on Eddy Street between Fillmore and Webster Streets, just two blocks away. The brick exterior of the top two floors of this five-story building fell to the ground, leaving the studs completely exposed. This type of destruction was common throughout the surrounding area and it took several years for the city to fully rebuild itself.

George's Mother Emma and the Earthquake Aftermath

I found no evidence to suggest George and his family ever returned to the Eddy Street house. At this point, in fact, my search for information on the family had gone cold. Finally, I found George listed in a 1908 Oakland City Directory living at 2918 Benvenue Avenue, but no trace of Emma or Rufus. I searched for clues in the 1910 US Census and finally found a scattered family and a shocking story: George was listed as a family member (nephew), living with his Uncle George Anderson, Emma's brother in Oakland, California. I found Rufus listed as a family member (nephew), living with his Aunt Millie Kline, Emma's sister, in Bodega, California. This same Census disclosed a Mrs. Emma Dawes as a patient in a state mental facility located in Stockton, California, about eighty miles away.

Until I started writing this report of investigation, I was never quite certain if this was George's mother. A second search for Emma produced medical records from that same state hospital in Stockton. Emma's commitment record was actually available online. The record revealed that on May 14, 1908, just one year after the earthquake, twenty-three-year-old George committed his mother to the state hospital for what was termed at the time "melancholia," a mental condition marked by persistent depression and ill-founded fears that can be triggered by stress. An entry on the commitment sheet identified "Stress of business and handling husband's estate" as a major factor. She was classified as suicidal.

After digging deeper into Emma's life, I realized this poor woman had dealt with stress and tragedy her whole life. The 1860 US Census indicated she was born in or about 1859, the third daughter of Benj (Benjamin) and Margt (Margaret) Kline, in San

Francisco. Older sisters Adelaide (Addie) and Amelia (Millie) were born in 1855 and 1857. In the 1870 Census, two more siblings appeared, a sister Mary born in 1866 and a brother George born in 1868. In this era, the age gap might suggest that Margaret had died sometime after Emma's birth and that Benjamin had remarried. However, with so few vital records to review from this period there was no way to know. I could not find any additional information for Margaret.

I did find further information on Benjamin in several *San Francisco City Directory* listings. From 1861 to '67 he was listed as a plasterer living near the corner of Vallejo and Montgomery Streets. I didn't find his name in the 1868 directory, however, "Mrs. Benjamin Kline (widow)" appeared in 1869. California death records reported the 1869 death of a Benjamin "Klein," whose birth year and location matched that of Benjamin Kline. Without other available documentation, I can only assume authorities at the time used a more common spelling for his last name. Even the city directories listed "Klein" and "Cline" as alternatives for Kline. If this was in fact Benjamin Kline, his death would have been a staggering blow, leaving Mrs. Kline (whether that be Margaret or another woman) alone with five children, ages one to fourteen. Her options must have been bleak.

The 1870 US Census listed Emma and her younger brother George living with their adoptive parents William and Sarah Anderson in the small community of San Rafael, outside of San Francisco. Addie was in a home that housed single women with young children. I found Millie living with Barbara Sims, the Anderson's former housekeeper. By 1880, Addie and Mary reunited with Emma and George as part of the Anderson household, with all changing their last name to Anderson. Millie remained with Barbara Sims and was the only sibling to maintain the original surname "Kline."

In 1884, at age twenty-five, Emma married Richard Cranch Dawes, a man twenty-two years her senior. Now living in comfort, in an exciting new city, she bore him two sons within the next three years only to become a widow eleven years later. She was left to raise her two young boys independently during a time when women had little standing in society. While Richard's estate provided her with a sizeable trust fund, the most devastating (in terms of cost and lives) earthquake in US history forced her out of her home of eighteen years. Worse yet, her adoptive father (William Anderson) died seven months after the earthquake. She was admitted to the state hospital soon after.

Mental illness was not an open topic for discussion at the turn of the twentieth century, causing much secret and painful suffering to many people. Further research into Emma's siblings left me wondering if such secrets were somehow hidden within the Kline DNA, since both of her sisters seemed to have followed a similar fate. The 1900 US Census identified Millie Kline as a member of the Dawes household on Eddy Street soon after Richard died.

Ten years later, the 1910 US Census reported her and Rufus as residents of Camp Meeker, a former logging camp located along the Russian River, about sixty miles north of San Francisco. Then, tragically, the 1920 US Census identified her as a patient in the Santa Clara State Mental Hospital for the Insane. That same year, Addie was listed as an "Inmate" at the San Francisco Relief Home, a facility originally designed to house refugees of the 1906 earthquake, but by this time taking in people needing long-term medical care. I have no idea what happened to Millie but I was relieved to learn from the 1930 US Census that at some point

Addie recovered enough to become a member of her sister Mary's household in San Rafael, where Mary had taken over their father's grocery store.

As an investigator, I routinely look for commonalities or patterns of behavior among subjects and witnesses. In this case, what should have been quite common for most women in the late 1800s was not common for the Kline women: with the exception of Emma, none of the Kline/Anderson sisters married or had children. George Anderson did marry but had no children. Perhaps these siblings were simply not up for the demands of parenthood, or perhaps they chose not to marry or have children out of fear of passing on a negative family trait.

After six years at the state hospital in Stockton, Emma was declared "recovered" and released on December 15, 1913. I am not certain who would have been responsible for her expenses (whether the State of California, George, or possibly an insurance company); however, her commitment papers reported that she had "personal property, valued at $7,000." Her transition back to normal life would not have been an easy one. Just one month later, her adoptive mother, Sarah Anderson, died.

Then the following spring, another tragedy struck. According to an article in the *Oakland Tribune*, from 1914:

WOMAN IS MISSING

SAN FRANCISCO March 28 – Mrs. Emma Dawes, 55 years of age, has been missing from her home at 1231 Thirty-seventh avenue. since March 20, and her friends and relatives are in despair over her absence. The case is in the hands of Detective Manuel de la Guerra, who is searching the city for her. She is 5 feet 3 inches in height, with dark hair. It is not known how she was dressed on the day she left home.

WOMAN IS MISSING.

SAN FRANCISCO March 28.— Mrs. Emma Dawes. 55 years of age, has been missing from her home, at 1231 Thirty-seventh avenue. since March 20, and her friends and relatives are in despair over her absence. The case is in the hands of Detective Manuel de la Guerra, who is searching the city for her. She is 5 feet 3 inches in height, with dark hair. It is not known how she was dressed on the day she left home.

Emma did not return home; she was never found. According to my mother, no one knew what became of her. After thirteen years of uncertainty, George had his mother, Emma (Anderson) Dawes declared legally dead. At the probate hearing, her estate was estimated to be worth $10,000 ($257,000 in today's currency).

George's Brother Rufus, on the Russian River

As the oldest son it fell to George to deal with his mother's mental state and he was also responsible for looking out for the welfare of his younger brother Rufus. Rufus considered himself a rancher and would often work on farms outside San Francisco. Sometime between 1906 and '10 he sustained a head injury from an accident involving a horse, leaving him unable to fully care for himself the rest of his life. As mentioned, the 1910 US Census placed Rufus with his Aunt Millie living at Camp Meeker. So, Millie was more than just his aunt; she had been his caregiver at times. This leaves me to believe Millie was the aunt noted in my mother's statement, "…it does seem that there may have been an aunt that he looked up to as I don't really remember him saying much about his father."

After having been decommissioned for logging, in 1898 Camp Meeker was subdivided into tiny lots, originally selling for $10 each. The area was used as a vacation spot for people from San Francisco, easily accessible by train. Sometime shortly after the turn of the twentieth century, Emma purchased at least three adjoining lots and built a small cottage they named, "Sweet Afton," where Rufus lived most of his adult life. Millie also owned property in Camp Meeker, making it easy for her to look after her nephew.

In his later years, George often spent weekends at Camp Meeker with Rufus. The brothers maintained the property well into the late 1950s. Here, according to my mother, "George's secretary sat for many years, used as two separate pieces because the ceilings were not tall enough to accommodate it." With the cottage already well established by 1906, I believe the secretary was moved out of the family home on Eddy Street immediately after the earthquake and into the family cottage where it remained until joining the Watts home in 1955.

Beyond what I knew from my family's personal connection, I first spotted George "in the wild" in the 1905 *San Francisco City Directory*. He was listed as a wood finisher for California Electrical Works of San Francisco. At this point in his life, about to gain complete access to his trust fund as an adult in March of the next year, the prospect of a financially secure future came, as we know, crashing down around him one month later when he and his family, like so many others, were devastated by the earthquake.

Before 1906, George hadn't attended college but at some point thereafter he took a training course in bookkeeping and accounting. Though we don't know whether he had always planned to follow in the footsteps of his father as a bookkeeper or if circumstance made the choice for him. In 1908 he emerged in an edition of the *Oakland City Directory* as a bookkeeper for an unidentified company.

By 1913 George was working as a clerk for the Marconi Wireless Telephone Company. He moved on to another bookkeeping position with Louis Winer in 1915. Finally, in 1919, with a few years of experience under his belt, George joined Gordon Rowe of San Francisco, a well-known accounting firm, where he worked as an auditor for the next thirty-five years.

Like his aunts and uncles, George had no children. He did not marry until he was well into his late thirties, in or about 1924, and his wife, Mary (Strong) Griffin, was a widow eight years older than he and well beyond childbearing years. I have often wondered if watching and caring for his mentally disabled mother and seeing similar tendencies in her siblings caused George to delay marriage and give up thoughts of fatherhood altogether.

Following the earthquake, and even after he met Mary, George rented various small residences in the Oakland area. Outside of the property in Camp Meeker inherited from his mother, he never owned a piece of property again. George and Mary finally returned to San Francisco around 1935, where she died five years later, at age sixty-four, of heart failure and an intestinal disorder.

George remained in the city until 1943, when he moved to Woodland for a new opportunity. A November 20, 1943, article in the *Sacramento Bee* "San Franciscan Is Given Yolo Position." George had been appointed accountant in the office of County

Auditor Fred Porter, after he aided an audit of the Yolo County books as an employee of Gordon Rowe of San Francisco. This corroborates my mother's story about meeting and working with George in Woodland, California. He resigned over a salary dispute with Yolo County a few years later and returned to Gordon Rowe, where he stayed until he retired in 1955. He then sold the Camp Meeker property and he and Rufus moved to a small apartment in Sacramento.

A Life Without Family

I am astounded to consider the events and social and technological developments this man personally witnessed during his lifetime. Think about this: in the year of his birth, Grover Cleveland had just won the 1884 Presidential election. The cornerstone of the Statute of Liberty was laid in New York and the Washington Monument was completed. Mark Twain wrote *The Adventures of Huckleberry Finn* and the Ringling Brothers Circus opened for the very first time.

As a boy, George must have heard stories about an invention that would allow people to talk to one another between distant cities. A few years later this same device would be installed at his family home. He had seen the first automobiles driving on the streets of San Francisco and he probably read about the Wright Brothers successful flight at Kitty Hawk in his morning newspaper. Then came radio, then television. Just imagine what he was thinking when he watched the astronauts blast off into space and return safely to earth. George did not just witness version upgrades to the latest technological gadget — he actually watched as original inventions changed the world and everyday life. (Will any generation ever witness this much change and advancement ever again?)

As exciting as the world must have been during those years, it could not soften the severe human tragedies that also impacted George's life. He lost his father at an early age. His family was completely displaced after the earthquake. Mental illness consumed and destroyed his mother and her sister Millie, and took a toll on her other sister. His brother suffered a debilitating brain injury as a young man. Personal tragedies aside, George also had to maneuver through and survive even bigger obstacles taking place in the world around him: a world pandemic (Spanish Flu), the stock market crash, the Great Depression, and two world wars. These were but of a few of the challenges he faced during the first half of the twentieth century, events that shook American society to its core. Many people did not survive. Those who did rarely shared their experiences with loved ones. I imagine talking about such personal tragedies would only bring up deeply buried memories, heartache, and sadness. Perhaps George avoided my mother's personal questions to spare himself from those distressing memories. But why not discuss his historic family?

After comparing George's timeline with those of his closest relatives, I realized there was another personal tragedy in the mix that must have weighed heavily on him his whole life. Like his mysterious secretary, George was missing a major part of his identity.

George had grown up in San Francisco, apart from his father's close-knit family, who had all lived in the Boston area before the turn of the twentieth century. With the exception of one uncle, all of these people and his own father were dead by the time George was fifteen. He and his brother soon became the last of this Dawes line. By the time he was old enough to become interested in his heritage, there was no one to confer with.

As a substitute for the personal stories he missed hearing from his father and grandparents, the Holland book provided him with a road map of his Dawes ancestors as far back as the seventeenth century. Other family books in the collection connected him to his Greenleaf and Cranch lines but family names do not keep one company during holiday affairs nor do they provide the human touch or the personality traits we grow to love or hate about our own family. In a sense, the Dawes Collection served as George's stand-in family, always present, always faithful, but never fully known or understood. Sadly, it also lacked the warmth and reassurance only a living soul can provide.

What I would give for one last afternoon with Mr. Dawes, to share with him all of my remarkable discoveries. But regarding his intentions: I seriously doubt that George ever intended to mislead or withhold information about his family and their personal belongings from my mother. Simply put, he could not tell her what he did not know.

George's father, Richard Cranch Dawes, circa 1878 (age 40)

7

The Evidence

Part II: Nanty's letters

What were the chances of Renee Daphne Kimball and I ever meeting had it not been for Nanty's letters? Absolutely zero.

We were both independent women who took on life and all its challenges but our pathways had led us in opposite directions: Renee lived in Portland, Oregon; I lived in Phoenix, Arizona. Renee was a free spirit, never afraid to explore uncharted seas with a sense of wonderment. She was not afraid to question authority or step over the line just a bit, and then organize a good debate about it; she was a "big picture" person, hopping from one project to the next, hoping to change and improve the world and never hesitating to share her opinion. I was a Special Agent, a follower and enforcer of rules. I focused on precise details and planning the next step, my opinion unspoken.

Sometimes I wish I could be more like Renee.

Renee and I had met online in 2000, through our inquiries about the Dawes family to the Quincy Historical Society. Five years before Renee received my email, she had purchased the intriguing collection of letters, written between 1843 and 1870 by a young woman called "Nanty," who mentioned various members of the Dawes family of Quincy. Renee expressed a strong desire to publish a book based on the letters; however, life caught up with her and she had yet to find the time to do so. My own goal was much simpler at that moment: I was just looking for evidence that might help identify who in George's family had once owned his secretary. When Renee had first told me about the collection of Nanty letters, I wasn't even sure if they were relevant to my investigation.

For some reason, Renee wanted Nanty's identity to remain a mystery to her for as long as possible, so she insisted I not reveal her true name should I discover it. Over the next seventeen years, during which Renee and I talked and emailed only rarely, I did wonder at times why she was so hesitant to learn of my significant discoveries and to share her own historical finds with me. The few times she did, it would spark renewed energy, igniting something inside both of us; but it was usually temporary, burning out within a few months.

But the few letters that Renee did share with me quickly helped me put the pieces together, so (in accordance with her wishes) I secretly knew Nanty's identity for years. However, I believed Renee and I would finally meet some day to share our information about Nanty's letters and the Dawes family, and that belief kept me reaching out to her every so often.

In October 2017, seventeen years after our initial introduction and after a three-year hiatus since our last contact, I emailed Renee to let her know I had returned to Phoenix. I mentioned my professional work would be ending within a year and that I was looking forward to finding a fun retirement project, my way of offering my services as a transcriber for any untouched Nanty letters.

Hearing nothing back, I began to wonder if Renee was still alive or if our Nanty-based relationship was now a thing of the past. Finally, two months later, Renee called me. She apologized for her delay, attributing her nonresponse of the last few years to health issues she had been dealing with.

I could tell my willingness to work on Nanty's letters sparked something inside her once again—this time with greater intensity. Renee's thoughts of writing a historic mystery novel were long gone by now; she was more interested in sharing the importance of original writings. She also wished to honor Nanty by bringing her life and artistic talents into public view. I was delighted to learn that. Due to my extensive knowledge of this particular line of the Dawes family, Renee wanted to collaborate with me on a new format for her book.

To give me a taste of what she had in mind, Renee sent a couple of Nanty's letters for me to transcribe (or try to). The handwriting was small and filled up every square inch of a page, spilling over onto the outer borders. The 1800s terminology was confusing at times. Challenging did not begin to describe this exercise: it was painful and frustrating beyond any casework I had ever experienced. No wonder Renee's own attempts were often sidelined in favor of other projects.

I was torn. I could see how the transcription project needed to be done on a full-time basis if we were to ever gain a full understanding of the writer's style and handwriting, but I did not have that kind of time to invest quite yet. I was still working part time for SIGAR and preparing for my final two cases to go to trial within months.

I think the idea of working on the Nanty project with someone as excited as she was about it was something nice for Renee to dwell on when she was suddenly surprised by the unwelcome news that as a breast cancer survivor, she may have some new cause for concern. About this time, I received word that my DC trial was postponed another six months. Suddenly, I had an open space on my calendar.

At long last, I flew to Portland to meet Renee.

Face-to-Face with Renee

Inside a small Taiwanese restaurant, a short little woman with long flowing grey hair embraced me in a bear hug and would not let go. This was Renee in the flesh. We never stopped talking the entire two days I was there.

This first restaurant encounter was just a meet and greet. We spent time over dinner finally getting to know each other, then tackled Nanty's letters in full force the following morning.

As soon as I stepped into Renee's home, I saw her kitchen table buried with everything Nanty. Like a mother hen hovering over newborn chicks, she carefully removed original letters and drawings from their protective binders, proudly presenting me with one after another. I was amazed and amused by Nanty's accounts of family and the people in her community over a span of twenty-seven years. But most impressive were the large pages of hand-drawn caricatures depicting everyday life in Quincy, Boston, New York, and Washington, DC. I could now match faces to family names as these people came to life inside their homes.

The kitchen table pulsated from the family chatter portrayed in the ongoing parties and family events. I was examining the full collection of Nanty's letters in their original form and by doing so I met George's extended family; his father, his uncles, his aunt, his grandparents, and even his great-grandparents were all there, and — in that moment — so alive. I witnessed how they lived their lives in the nineteenth century. Mesmerized with each new letter and image Renee placed before me, I felt like I was on surveillance again, having found the perfect vantage point to watch and learn about all my subjects. This was not just one bizarre and unbelievable incident, it was a never ending stampede of chills and thrills throughout the entire day.

Many drawings depicted scenes inside the Cranch Greenleaf House. I could not believe how much detail Nanty provided: the food, the furniture, and even men and women's fashion. But what about George's secretary? Was it there? Renee was sure she had seen it (or one like it) in one of the drawings but she could not locate that particular drawing among the hundred or so sheets laid out on the table.

Though we didn't find it before I departed, Renee had a massive surprise waiting for me: She took out a small, yellowed envelope that had been addressed to Mary Greenleaf Stallknecht, Nanty's cousin. Inside, an old photograph of a woman peeked out from under the flap. I immediately recognized the woman's hair style and mouth—that oversized mouth she always drew in scenes she was part of. I was looking at a true image of Nanty. I could no longer keep the secret. I introduced Renee to George's Aunt. Mary Elizabeth (Dawes) Mitchell, also known as "Nanty."

Inside a carefully folded piece of paper I found something even more personal to Nanty than her stitch sampler: a strand of golden-brown hair and a small braided hair ring, a common nineteenth-century keepsake, created as part of the mourning process. Both were almost 150 years old, yet perfectly preserved. That familiar chill raced up and down my spine.

The thought of finally working with Renee on this project was very exciting but, unfortunately, within days of our meeting, Renee received concerning news from her doctors. Her cancer was back and she had a fight on her hands. Just like that, Renee's focus shifted entirely to her treatment plan. While my work pulled me in the opposite direction: the defendant in my Phoenix case decided to go to trial instead of taking a plea, surprising us all. We were left to quickly prepare for a trial that lasted two weeks. Two days after the verdict came in, I boarded a plane for

Italy to do witness interviews for my DC trial, now scheduled to take place in five short weeks. My part-time status suddenly changed to full-time and then some. The DC trial lasted three grueling weeks, concluding just three days before my contract with SIGAR ended.

By October 1st, I was fully retired once again and ready to start transcribing Nanty's letters. In the meantime, Renee was tackling a nontraditional treatment plan, which she hoped would be easier and more effective than the traditional treatments she tried years earlier. Renee was a positive thinker. She believed attitude played a vital role in the recovery process.

We soon began biweekly phone calls. Discussions of Nanty's letters would inevitably launch into other topics, so many other topics. I loved that I could always express my opinions to Renee. No matter how much our views were opposed, she never offered any criticism. "And why do you think that?" she would ask, such a great question when trying to understand different viewpoints. Best of all, we laughed a good bit. And sometimes we would remember the point of what we were doing and get back to one obvious, nagging question: how had Nanty's letters found their way to a used bookstore in Portland?

Tracing the Letters' Chain of Custody

Making little progress on that question, I decided to put my extensive investigative experience to work figuring out the basic W's—the who, what, where, why (and, in this case, how)—regarding the letters' chain of custody.

Nanty's last letter was written just before she died in January 1870. Most were addressed to her cousin "Bones" (Lucy and Harrison Daweses' oldest child). Bones had completed her schooling in Quincy and, with no marriage prospects, travelled to Lowell to live with and help her relatives the Nortons. In 1847 she moved to Washington, DC, near other members of the Cranch and Greenleaf families. As an unmarried woman living in a city like DC, she would have needed their support and guidance. I was surprised to learn that Bones had become a career woman, working for the US Department of the Treasury as a clerk for almost twenty years. For many of those, Nanty's letters kept Bones informed about friends and family and the news in Quincy.

In 1879 a Brookline, Massachusetts, directory showed Bones living in the home of her aunt Mary Dawes and cousin George. The 1880 US Census confirmed this same living arrangement. By this time, Mary's husband George Minot Dawes and sister Lucy Dawes were both deceased. Presumably, Bones retained the collection of Nanty's letters until her death in Brookline in 1884.

Nanty's letters were then passed down as cherished items by her family members: her caricatures provided a family album before photographs were commonplace. Who would have taken possession of the letters after Bones died? Personal items like these were typically passed down through the female members of a family but Bones had never married, never had children.

Her sisters were the next logical choice. Looking at her branch of the family tree, I identified two possibilities, Mary Greenleaf Dawes and Margaret Cranch Dawes. Both were extremely close to Nanty and often mentioned and drawn in her letters for good reason. They, Bones, their three brothers, and their mother Lucy (Greenleaf) Dawes, all moved into the Cranch Greenleaf House in 1835, relocating from Baltimore after their father, Harrison Dawes, died unexpectedly.

Since the two Dawes brothers — Harrison and George — had married Greenleaf sisters, Lucy's family genealogy was identical to the one I had already created for Mary. However, family ancestors were not going to help me find a Portland connection. My focus needed to be on Lucy's descendants: I had identified her children, it was now time to populate the family tree with Lucy's grandchildren and great-grandchildren and to establish a possible pathway to Portland, where in 1995 Renee would discover Nanty's letters tucked away in a display case of the Great Northwest Bookstore. Ancestry's family tree program and search feature became my two best friends and colleagues.

Given the custom of passing personal belongings down through the female side of the family, I decided to focus on just the women of this family and their descendants:

- *Lucy "Bones" Cranch Dawes:* Bones never married and was childless; her line ended with her.

- *Mary Greenleaf (Dawes) Stallknecht:* Mary married Frederic Stallknecht in 1844 and moved to New York. They had four sons and a daughter, Josepha, who never married or had children and remained in the New York area. Another line ended.

- *Margaret Cranch (Dawes) Ripley:* This is the same Margaret Ripley who was associated with the Adams/Cranch japanned high chest that sold at auction in 1999 for $1.6 million. She married Lyman Ripley in 1858 and moved to St. Louis. She had four sons and two daughters.

- *Nellie Howard (Ripley) Wallace:* Margaret's oldest daughter married Edwin Wallace and lived a very social life in Pennsylvania. She had four daughters who all stayed true to their Pennsylvania roots. I found no connection to Portland here.

- *Lucy Greenleaf (Ripley) Joy:* Margaret's youngest daughter married Wilford Joy in 1894 and lived in St. Louis for many years, though the 1910 US Census for St. Louis identified Wilford Joy as divorced. Divorce is never a dead end when trying to find someone, it's just the beginning of a new life, so I searched the 1920 US Census and found Lucy living with her brother John Ripley in—of all places—Portland, Oregon. (A true bizarre and unbelievable incident and a long overdue reward but one that did not, unfortunately, prove anything.) Lucy and Wilford had no children.

- *Margaret G. (Ripley) Wakeman:* Lucy's brother John Ripley had a son and a daughter, Margaret, who married Henry Wakeman. They had three daughters who also grew up in Portland. Margaret died in 1985, the same year the Great Northwest Bookstore acquired the letters (although it is possible the letters had been left a few years earlier). I was not sure if this was a significant find or a mere coincidence.

Old-School Techniques

The expanded family tree and my timeline matched up perfectly, adding weight to my theory that Nanty's letters had been passed down through this female line, generation to generation, until reaching Margaret Wakeman's hands. But though it appeared to be an excellent theory, I had no way of knowing whether it was anywhere close to the truth. I needed a night or two for this new-found information to sit on a back burner and simmer for a while.

My memory had not failed me, it was just stuck in neutral, buried under twelve years of newer data. Thank goodness for the old-school techniques and training that ensured I kept everything in the case file. I dug back into my document collection and found the auction information sheet Sotheby's had sent me about the japanned high chest of drawers given to Mary Cranch by John Adams. It read,

> According to family tradition the present high chest of drawers was owned at one time by John Adams. In 1788, he presented the chest to his sister-in-law, Mary (Smith) Cranch of Quincy, Massachusetts, with the descent of the chest through the family as follows:
>
> - Mary Cranch
> - Lucy (Cranch) Greenleaf
> - Lucy (Greenleaf) Dawes
> - Margaret Greenleaf (Dawes) Ripley
> - Lucy Greenleaf (Ripley) Joy
> - John Dawes Ripley
> - Margaret Greenleaf (Ripley) Wakeman
> - Current owners (Margaret's daughters)

This bizarre and unbelievable incident was dramatically upgraded to an OSOD discovery with outburst. This was the identical path I had just traced and theorized about for how Nanty's letters moved from Massachusetts to Portland. What better place to store these cherished letters than inside the japanned high chest as it was passed down from one generation to the next?

With this discovery came another significant realization, the reason this separate piece of furniture was so important to my investigation. The japanned high chest had descended from Mary Cranch to her daughter Lucy (Cranch) Greenleaf and, just like George's secretary, it hadn't left the Cranch Greenleaf House until the two Greenleaf/Dawes sisters and their families moved out around 1857 after their parents, John and Lucy Greenleaf, died. The two pieces had been housemates for over sixty years.

But when it was time to separate their parents' and grandparents' belongings, Mary Cranch's japanned high chest went with Lucy and then descended primarily (unless there were no daughters) through the female line.

Incredibly, these two pieces have withstood the challenges of time (well over 230 years) and countless moves, yet each remains carefully preserved and well cared for. It seemed logical to assume Richard Cranch's secretary had gone to Lucy's sister Mary, then through one of her son's lines, since her only daughter predeceased her. And who better to receive Richard Cranch's secretary than his great-grandson and namesake—Richard Cranch Dawes—George's father?

How the Letters Landed at the Great Northwest Bookstore

Feeling quite confident about how Nanty's letters had gotten to Portland, we were still left with the question of why this cherished collection of family letters had ended up in a used bookstore. Unfortunately, Margaret and her daughters were no longer available for interviews. Whatever facts they might have known followed them to their graves.

Further research led me to an article printed in a local Portland newspaper in 1999 regarding the japanned high chest after the auction. Margaret's daughters—the owners of the piece at that time—had no idea of the high chest's value, until one of them attended a museum lecture on American furniture. According to the article, these women hadn't been able to give the chest away, no one had wanted it. Imagine living with a historic piece of furniture never knowing its true value! I bet the entire audience at that auction could hear their OSOD outburst when the hammer price stood at $1.6 million.

It was now May 2019, and Renee's health was not going well. One day, she dropped an unexpected bombshell, announcing, "I am sending the collection of Nanty's letters to you."

What do you say when someone tells you they are entrusting you with something they cherish more than anything else in the world? I felt like I was on a parallel course with my mother, understanding for the first time how she must have felt when George left his secretary and family treasures with her. I agreed to become the caretaker for her treasured gift but the thrill of taking on this awesome responsibility was overshadowed by the realization that Renee was finally giving up her well-fought battle against cancer. I promised to make her dream of publishing Nanty's letters a reality, and we spent the next few weeks discussing what a future book should look like.

Renee knew that by entrusting the collection to me it would be reunited with Nanty's stitch sampler and George's secretary. Think about it: George's secretary sat for years in the parlor of the Cranch Greenleaf House, so Nanty had grown up seeing it. She may have even written one of her letters on its desktop. Renee also knew I would be looking for a new home for George's secretary at some point and that I would find the right place for Nanty's letters as well.

On August 2, 2019, a gigantic box arrived at my doorstep via UPS. I immediately texted Renee to let her know everything had arrived intact. "OMG, Christmas in August!" I added.

"Have a wonderful day and we will talk soon," she wrote back. Sadly, we never did. Renee lost her courageous battle five days later.

Reviewing the Collection

Over the following four months I dedicated my time and energy to transcribing every letter and caricature within the collection. I needed to do this exercise to figure out what was in the collection and to keep my commitment to Renee. The thought of creating a product suitable for publishing completely intimidated me. I had no skills for such a daunting project. I knew of no one in the publishing world. I had no idea how to start.

Even so, I felt I owed it to Renee to try. And there was one more undeniably motivating factor: it would be the perfect opportunity to look for more clues about George's secretary.

Renee had cautiously and painstakingly stored each document in its own acid-free protector and then, depending on its size, carefully placed each one in an appropriately sized scrapbook. Working with these original documents was forbidden; my first step would be to scan the whole collection and create a numbering system for easy retrieval, one for the letters and another for the drawings.

As mentioned, most of the letters were addressed to Nanty's cousin Bones. But this full accounting of the collection laid out before me made it obvious that she was also the caretaker of other cherished family letters from previous generations. There were forty letters in all, twenty-nine written by Nanty, the remaining eleven by other family members, including Bones, Mary and Lucy (Greenleaf) Dawes, and their brother William Greenleaf.

One Special Letter

One letter in particular caught my eye: It was by far the oldest and, in fact, the most significant in the collection. I removed the letter from its protective sleeve: a single page, as was common in the 1800s or before, when a page would be folded to a certain size with the writing facing inward so that the addressee's name could be written on the opposite side, on what became the envelope.

As I placed it on the scanner face down, I noticed the addressee's name written on the back, "William Cranch, Esq., Haverhill." I immediately flipped the page over to see the original date. "April 12th, Saturday night." That was the only clue. There was no formal salutation, only the words from a lovestruck woman who signed her name simply as "Lucy." The partial remains of a red-wax seal still clung to the brittle yellowed page. This was a letter written by Lucy Cranch, Richard Cranch's daughter, to her brother William prior to her marriage to her fiancé John Greenleaf. William was married to John's sister, Anna "Nancy" (Greenleaf) Cranch. In the letter, Lucy wrote of her devoted love and affection for John and his family even though John's blindness was a wavering issue for her own. The two finally wed on April 4, 1795. An Internet search pulled up a 1794 calendar confirming April 12th fell on a Saturday that year. It's no exaggeration to say I was a bit awestruck realizing I was holding an original letter written 225 years earlier, while George Washington served as the first President of the United States.

Scanning the drawings came next: sixty pages of caricatures, though some pages contained numerous "scenes" complete with dialogue bubbles. I noticed one major consistency throughout the collection, Nanty always drew herself somewhere in each scene. Many of Nanty's letters also included caricatures but I sensed these larger ones were done more as standalone drawings, which could be passed around between family members without needing a letter to explain what was happening.

With everything scanned, the horrid job of transcription could no longer be postponed. It was by far the most arduous task I ever performed during an investigation. Trying to transcribe 150-year-old handwriting crammed into a space meant for half as many words tried my patience. Figuring out what was written in the caricature conversation bubbles was even more frustrating. Sometimes it was just a phrase or—even more difficult—Nanty often used mid-1800s jargon that I did not understand. Google became my research partner for history lessons on the various vintage words and phrases I came across.

Throughout this process I continually questioned the need for such an exercise, wondering if it was really worth it. But these newly scanned images grounded me. They could be enlarged for better review (though even magnified three times larger than the original, there were still many words I could not decipher). Finally, I transcribed the last letter. I had a new sense of accomplishment, but I knew the next step would be to put these events of Nanty's life story in order.

Tackling Nanty's Timeline

Renee's filing system, which simply placed each letter and drawing into a scrapbook, did little to help me fully understand Nanty's life journey and family. With my analytical mind kicking into high gear, along with an overwhelming desire to connect all the related people and events, I soon realized nothing in the collection was in any particular order: not by place, not by date, and, with the exception of one group of scenes, none of the drawings seemed to match up with any of the stories mentioned in the letters. To bring order and insight to this hodgepodge of people and events, I needed to rely once again on my favorite investigative tool, the timeline.

The full collection of letters started in 1794, with Lucy Cranch's letter to her brother William and ended in 1874, with a letter Bones sent to her sister Mary Stallknecht four years after Nanty died. Every other letter or caricature fit somewhere in between these two.

Starting with the letters, I laid out those with full dates appearing next to the salutation and placed them in order. Next, I dealt with the letters with partial dates, much like the Lucy Cranch letter. With the help of old calendars, it was not difficult to figured out which year a certain date fell on. Once I had the complete date identified, I inserted the letter into its rightful place on the timeline. Despite a few stragglers with no hint of a date, and having transcribed all of the letters, I gained a feel for what was happening at certain times. And by reviewing the written contents, I had an at least partially informed idea as to where on the timeline the letter belonged.

Inserting the drawings between the letters on this same timeline was trickier. Only a handful of the drawings had dates. But since Nanty always drew herself in each scene as she appeared at the time of the drawing, it was easy to estimate dates of caricatures drawn in her pre-adult days. Same for drawings illustrating her younger siblings, George, Richard, and Ambrose.

The adult images were another challenge. Fortunately, as I continued reviewing the drawings, patterns and common elements started revealing themselves. Many of the drawings included scenes taking place in New York City, Boston, and Washington, DC. Others provided views of the Cranch Greenleaf House in Quincy, both inside and out. I noticed the same family members in these various locations. Judge William Cranch and his sons William and John, Bones, Uncle Rufus Dawes, and Uncle William Greenleaf all lived in DC. Mary (Dawes) Stallknecht, Nanty's cousin, lived with her husband Frederic and their children in New York. Nanty's Uncle Richard Greenleaf and his family lived in Boston, with a summer home in Jamaica Plain.

When the time-period of a scene completely stumped me, I asked myself two key questions: based on what I had learned so far, what would have happened before this scene and what would have happened after? This created a placeholder on the timeline for the document in question, my best guess you might say. Not surprisingly, gaps began to fill in quite nicely even though I knew I would need to make adjustments later.

Fraud investigators are always looking for patterns of activity to help pull the datapoints of a case together, allowing us to connect all the shifting but relevant dots. Once connected, those dots can easily expose the fraud scheme. In this case, a true story about Nanty's life in Quincy, Boston, New York, and Washington, DC, emerged: Nanty obviously had a strong family network, her reason for spending months at a time in each city.

The more time I spent reviewing this collection of images, the more familiar I became with each of the family members. I was now expanding to three generations of Cranches, Greenleafs, and Daweses and, in many cases, when I placed the historic photographs of family members next to Nanty's caricature of the person, the match was recognizable. Now it was my kitchen island covered with everything Nanty, buzzing with conversations from all the family gatherings and community events laid out on top. I was no longer on surveillance peeking in from a window; I was inside these homes in my new undercover role, addressing all the players (the family members) by their first names.

I found the caricatures of Nanty's great uncle, Judge William Cranch, Esq., of particular interest. Judge Cranch had served as a judge for the circuit court of the District of Columbia (the first of three judges to fill such a position) from 1801 to '06 and as Chief Judge from 1806 until his death in 1855. His portrait still hangs inside a public display case seen as you enter the US Courthouse. There was never a problem picking him out of a lineup of Nanty's caricatures.

Judge William Cranch, 1844
Nanty's detail, circa 1852

Prior to leaving SIGAR, my last trial had taken place in this very courthouse; I walked by the display case with the judge's picture each morning on my way to the courtroom. Add another bizarre and unbelievable incident to the list.

My hours spent reviewing Nanty's letters proved invaluable in other ways as well. If you recall the first caricature Renee had sent me, entitled "Final Scene in the Front Parlor at Cranch Hall," I identified it as the day the family left the Cranch Greenleaf House in 1856 or '57. Yes, I admit it. I misidentified it. I broke

Investigation 101 rules by jumping to a conclusion before gathering all the facts, and I missed obvious clues. This could have been quite embarrassing had I tried to use this misidentified drawing as evidence in a trial. I am sure the defense council would have used it to discredit my investigative skills.

As it turns out, Cranch Hall did not mean the same thing as the "Cranch Greenleaf House." In one of Nanty's letters (written from Quincy) to Bones (living in Washington, DC), she asks what the family at "Cranch Hall" would be doing for Thanksgiving. I had overlooked obvious clues like the names of the newspapers scattered on the floor, representing publications from Alexandria, Virginia, and Washington, DC, during the mid-1800s. There was also a comment about Margie Brooks, the judge's daughter. So, the caricature actually depicted a scene from inside Judge Cranch's DC home. The judge's eldest son, William, stayed on in Cranch Hall for many years after the judge died in 1855. This scene depicts the last hours his family spent there, sometime around 1865.

Inching Closer to the Clincher

Something else interesting happened during this review process. I was examining every scanned scene with my investigator's eye, searching for additional clues, and making mental notes of questionable people, items, or places I saw. I discovered two scenes that were terribly similar, as if Nanty had drawn the same one twice, for some reason, and it caused me to take a closer look at both to identify the differences. Then my heart stopped. There was an object in one drawing that did not appear in the other. Practically hidden within the scene itself is a desk and bookcase, otherwise known as a secretary. An OSOD discovery times ten followed by a loud outburst and that now well-choreographed happy dance. Could this be the "clincher" Robert Mussey jokingly said I needed? Was it the proof I was searching for to connect Richard Cranch to George's secretary?

Multiple scenes by Nanty (including a secretary), circa 1845

Unfortunately, this drawing was not one of Nanty's more detailed renderings. The scene is inside the Cranch Greenleaf House in about 1845, before Lucy and John Greenleaf died (1846 and 1848). It serves as evidence that there was a Boston-style secretary in the Cranch Greenleaf House, one that looks remarkably similar to George's secretary — but is it George's?

Most agents would have closed the investigation at this point. However, after spending so much time reviewing all the drawings in the collection, I now knew all of the family members to the point of feeling like one of the family, one who had grown up in the Cranch Greenleaf House with the other cousins, one who had seen George's secretary and its housemate, the japanned high chest on a daily basis. In my mind, there was still one outstanding lead to pursue.

Nanty's rendering of George's secretary?

Pursuing One Last Lead

I reached back into my files to review the auction sales sheet for the japanned high chest Sotheby's sent me back in 2007. Hidden away on page four I came across this previously forgotten sentence, "A family history of the chest written in 1908 by Margaret Cranch (Dawes) Ripley, a great-granddaughter of Richard and Mary Cranch and the fourth member of the family to own the chest...."

There was a written history about the high chest, the house-mate to George's secretary for at least sixty years. Perhaps this document—a family document—could be my "Hail Mary" or, in this case, a "Hail Margaret," connecting Cranch to George's secretary. After all, Margaret had grown up in the Cranch Green-leaf House seeing both the high chest and George's secretary in whichever rooms they occupied. Was it possible she had also mentioned her great-grandfather's secretary in the document, while disclosing how family items were to be divided between her mother and Aunt Mary? I needed a copy of that document.

By now, in July 2020, twenty years had passed since the Chipstone Foundation had purchased the japanned high chest. I contacted Executive Director Jonathan Prown and explained my interest in their piece. I asked if they might have a copy of the high chest's history written by Margaret (Dawes) Ripley. Unfortunately, they did not, but Mr. Prown copied me on an email he sent to Sotheby's requesting the document. I laughed when I saw the email's Sotheby addressee: Erik Gronning, the associate who first sent me information about the high chest in 2007. Considering all the other bizarre and unbelievable incidents associated with this case, I should not have been surprised.

Erik was more than willing to help me out. He said the document I was looking for would be located in the original sales file, stored in the bowels of Sotheby's archives. There was just one (major) problem. COVID-19 was upon us and ravishing New York City. The archive office was completely shut down.

Being a researcher himself, Erik understood the importance of finding this document. It was my last outstanding lead, something I needed to check off my list even if the information failed to provide positive results. He promised to stay connected until things reopened and the document could be obtained. Nothing about this investigation moved quickly, not back in 2000 when I first began and certainly not during COVID. However, there was an upside to this worldwide lockdown: I had nothing but undisturbed time on my hands. First to review my investigative findings, and then to begin drafting this report of investigation. My "Hail Margaret" could remain in limbo until I was ready to write the last chapter.

Finally, in May 2021, Erik called, excitement in his voice. The archive offices were open and he had just received a number of boxes in response to his request. He wanted me to be part of the discovery process so we spoke on video chat. For the first time in thirteen years I had a face to go with the name. Erik held the phone over the first box allowing me to watch as he rummaged through the files looking for the name of the consignee. Nothing. Then the second box, nothing. Within a few minutes, he realized Archives sent the wrong boxes. I could only laugh, what else was there to do? Erik's assistant made a call to Archives, who assured them the correct boxes would be delivered soon.

Erik called two weeks later. He sounded almost giddy as he said, "Carleen, I have the right box sitting in front of me and I just need to find your document."

Within the hour I was looking at a copy of Margaret's historic document. It did not seem real. There is nothing more authentic than a letter or statement written by a family member or someone who personally witnessed an event. History textbooks fail to compare. As I read Margaret's story about the japanned high chest, I felt like I was reviewing another item found within Nanty's letters. This is how we should learn about our history — from the people who lived it, complete with their own slant or understanding of how things worked in their time and why they made the choices they did, whether we agree with those choices today or not.

Margaret recalled details that were told to her by her mother and grandmother about her great-grandfather Richard Cranch's relationship with his best friend John Adams. She reported that both Richard and Mary Cranch, who died one day apart, were buried on the same day in the Greenleaf tomb "in the little cemetery opposite the church." That would be Hancock Cemetery, where the Dawes family rests together. It is interesting to note that Margaret's account of which tomb Richard and Mary were buried in differs from Paul Nagel's (he reported they were in the Adams tomb). Either way, it is reassuring to know these families took care of one another from cradle to grave.

The japanned high chest (or "Chinese Chest of Drawers," as Margaret referred to it) came into the Cranch home as early as 1788. Margaret remembered seeing it when she was little, in her grandmother Greenleaf's room. After her death, it was always in her mother's room, in Quincy, in Roxbury, and in Brookline, where she died.

Did Margaret mention Richard Cranch's secretary?

Not one word.

8

The Closing Arguments

During this prolonged, arduous, and constantly inter-rupted investigation, I exposed and explored every imaginable lead and rabbit hole to solve the mystery of who in George's family had once owned his secretary. I interviewed George's closest friend. I consulted with expert witnesses with impeccable credentials in the study of eighteenth-century American furniture. I reviewed countless historical records from the county courthouses and public records of Massachusetts. I even developed and illustrated an extensive network of George's most closely associated family members, spanning 200 years and four generations.

A Special Agent's job is to collect admissible evidence to prove or disprove allegations of a criminal violation and to present all findings, positive or negative, to a prosecutor who will then decide whether the case has prosecutive merit. If, after all the painstaking work is completed, the case passes the prosecutor's review and is accepted for prosecution, it will then be presented to a Grand Jury. Having a case fail a prosecutor's review and be declined is a Special Agent's worst professional nightmare.

As an agent I was used to working on criminal and civil cases. As mentioned, the case against Richard Cranch is not criminal. However, if there was a federal violation for once owning an eighteenth-century secretary, was my evidence strong enough? Would it meet the burden of proof for a guilty verdict by a jury in a criminal trial? In other words, was it enough to lead twelve members of a jury to believe "beyond a shadow of a doubt" that Richard Cranch had once owned George's secretary?

I found no direct evidence linking Cranch to the secretary: no signature on a piece of wood hidden somewhere within a drawer or side wall, no original sales receipt, no directive in his will, or letter written by a family member specifically mentioning which family member had received the piece after Cranch died.

Based on this lack of evidence, the case would not have made it to trial; a declination by a prosecutor would be imminent.

However, the issue in this case is simply about ownership and provenance—the chain of custody—of a historic piece of furniture. Therefore, we would be accurate considering it as a civil issue and, as such, the burden of proof would not be as high. In such cases, only a "preponderance of the evidence" needs to be presented to a jury for them to decide on a guilty verdict.

How would a jury rule on this case? Does the "preponderance of evidence" suggest that it was more likely than not Richard Cranch had once owned George's secretary?

I invite you to take a seat in the jury box and listen to the closing arguments. Then it is up to you to decide.

Ladies and gentlemen of the jury, this case is quite simple. It is about reestablishing the historic provenance of an eighteenth-century mahogany secretary, lost due to time and family distance. The evidence clearly shows that "George's secretary" was once owned by Richard Cranch, best friend of President John Adams and brother-in-law to his wife, Abigail.

You heard testimony from expert witnesses Brock Jobe and Erik Gronning, who both specialize in American antique furniture from the eighteenth century. Although neither could identify the cabinetmaker by name, they agree George's secretary was made in Boston sometime between 1750 and '60.

Special Agent Carleen Watts testified to obtaining probate records from Norfolk County in Massachusetts for Richard Cranch that listed "1 desk and bookcase" — otherwise known as a secretary — on an inventory of household goods taken at the Cranches' Quincy, Massachusetts, home, otherwise known as the Cranch Greenleaf House. This established that Cranch did own a secretary at the time of his death in October 1811.

Agent Watts also showed you a timeline tracing the residences of various Cranch, Greenleaf, and Dawes family members from 1790 through 1972, and specifically highlighted those who had once lived in the Cranch Greenleaf House and when. The family maintained a continuous presence in this home from 1790 through 1856 or '57, starting with Cranch and continuing with his daughter Lucy Greenleaf and followed by her two daughters, Lucy (Greenleaf) Dawes and Mary E. (Greenleaf) Dawes.

Agent Watts further testified to receiving the collection of Nanty's letters from Renee Daphne Kimball, who purchased the collection from the Great Northwest Bookstore in Portland, Oregon, in 1995. Mary "Nanty" E. (Dawes) Mitchell, Richard Cranch's great-granddaughter, wrote these letters between 1843 and '70. Mrs. Mitchell grew up in the Cranch Greenleaf House, where she maintained her residency until she married in 1854. Her letters included drawings of family gatherings in the Cranch Greenleaf House. In one such drawing (circa 1845), a secretary appears in one of the main rooms of the home, clearly indicating such a piece was in the Cranch Greenleaf House while her grandparents, John and Lucy Greenleaf, were still alive.

Agent Watts showed you a link chart — a family tree connecting George Dawes to his great-great-grandfather Richard Cranch through his father, Richard Cranch Dawes, his mother Mary E (Greenleaf) Dawes, her mother Lucy (Cranch) Greenleaf, and finally her father Richard Cranch.

Agent Watts testified to finding several vintage silver pieces in a collection of family items once owned by George Dawes. The collection included five teaspoons engraved with the initials "RMC," indicating the original owners were Richard and Mary Cranch, George's great-great-grandparents. And three larger serving spoons engraved with the initials "JLG" indicating the original owners were John and Lucy Greenleaf, George's great-grandparents. The fact that George owned these items establishes and illustrates the family practice of handing down keepsakes to succeeding generations. In this case, the items were handed down from Mary Cranch to Lucy (Cranch) Greenleaf to Lucy's daughter, Mary (Greenleaf) Dawes, to her son, Richard Cranch Dawes, and then to his son, George Dawes.

This practice of descent is further supported by another piece of furniture found in the Cranch Greenleaf House, a housemate to George's secretary, the japanned high chest given to Mary Cranch by John Adams. In a document written in 1908 by Margaret (Dawes) Ripley, Richard Cranch's great-granddaughter, Margaret recalls living in the Cranch Greenleaf House and seeing the high chest in her grandmother's room until she died. It was then moved to her mother's room. When the family vacated the family home in 1856 or '57, her mother, Lucy (Greenleaf) Dawes, took possession, moving it from place to place until her death, at which time Margaret took possession. According to sales documents provided by Sotheby's auction house, the chest continued to descend to family members until its sale at auction in 1999.

Gloria Ann Watts, a trusted friend of George Dawes for more than forty years and Agent Watts's mother, testified before this court stating George gave her his family treasures, including his cherished secretary, in 1955 for her to safeguard and enjoy. Mrs. Watts watched over George and his affairs until his death in 1972 and served as caretaker of the Dawes Collection until 1995 when ownership passed on to her daughter, Agent Watts.

Although George Dawes could not appear before this court, Mrs. Watts also testified to hearing George's memory of being at the shipping docks in San Francisco as a young child with his father, Richard Cranch Dawes, to receive a shipment of family treasures from Boston, including the secretary, sent sometime between 1888 and '94, indicating Richard's mother, Mary (Greenleaf) Dawes possessed George's secretary until her death in 1886.

Ladies and gentlemen of the jury, I would also like to remind you of the victim in this case: "George's secretary," which, over the centuries, lost its true identity and claim to history. Finding Richard Cranch guilty of once owning George's secretary would reestablish this majestic old piece's distinguished provenance and link to its historic family.

And now, when Agent Watts looks at George's secretary and wonders, "Who once owned you?" she might finally hear its whispered response:
"I once belonged to Richard Cranch."

Mary E. "Nanty" Dawes Mitchell, possibly late teens

9

The Conclusion

A few months after receiving Nanty's letters, having scanned and carefully transcribing each page, I stood before George's secretary one morning thinking about the many unimaginable discoveries I had uncovered over the past twenty years. I would like to believe Nanty had sat at that desk to write or draw at least one of her many letters and caricature scenes. Her stitch sampler still hangs in my home on an adjacent wall from George's secretary along with pictures of George, his brother Rufus, his father Richard C. Dawes, and the old Cranch Greenleaf House.

My thoughts returned to the afternoon I spent at Hancock Cemetery in 2002 visiting the resting Dawes family and how I had unknowingly found myself standing next to Nanty's grave, the one with the headstone engraved with the name "Mary E. (Dawes) Mitchell." I wondered if that powerful and mysterious aura I felt as I paid my respects to this loving family was something deeper. Perhaps Nanty's spirit had reached out to me, letting me know our paths would cross again in the not-so-distant future. Perhaps it was the entire Dawes family letting me know they had chosen me to tell their story, guiding Nanty's letters to my doorstep and into my life for safekeeping.

If so, why me?

The answer was straightforward: I am a highly trained and skilled investigator with a heart for old things. I knew George, the last-surviving member of their family line. Like George, his father Richard, and his grandmother Mary, that same eighteenth-century mahogany secretary has been a part of my life from birth. And, like them, I now serve as its caretaker. Who is better suited to bring this family's story to life?

I believe there is a special power hidden within George's secretary that somehow allows each of its caretakers to build everlasting bonds with their predecessor. Mary Dawes probably took thoughts and memories of her mother Lucy with her when leaving the family home in Quincy for the last time. Richard Cranch Dawes must have felt the presence of his mother and family when the piece arrived in San Francisco. George was reminded of the father he barely knew each time he walked into his home. And, through their lasting friendship, my mother, Ann Watts, provided this same quiet, humble old man with a family he never had. As for me, the bond is just as personal.

While I was completing my original manuscript my mother passed away. She was ninety-four and suffered from dementia that eroded her memory over time. Connecting with someone in later stages of this disease is extremely difficult, and as a family member it can be heart-breaking. So, it's wonderful to connect over shared memories from their past that spark their brains. Musicians might be excited to hear a certain song, allowing them to briefly perform as they once did. In my mother's case, mentioning George and his secretary ignited that spark. Her face would light up and she would engage in meaningful conversation about items in the Dawes Collection. She took great delight in hearing about all of my discoveries, even if I repeated the same stories every few days.

This will forever be my most cherished gift from Mr. Dawes.

I hope the Dawes family is pleased with my investigative findings. As I once wrote at the end of hundreds of Reports of Investigation during my career: "Based on the foregoing information, this case is now closed."

Gloria "Ann" Watts
with George's secretary (2011)

APPENDIX A
The Dawes Family Tree

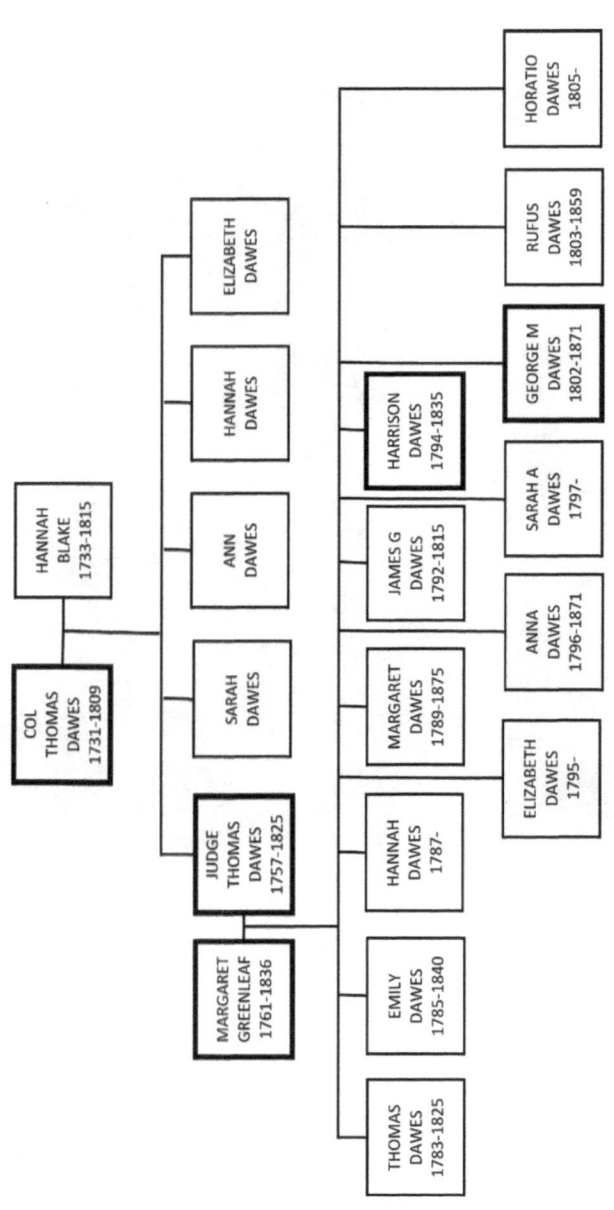

APPENDIX B
The Cranch Family Tree

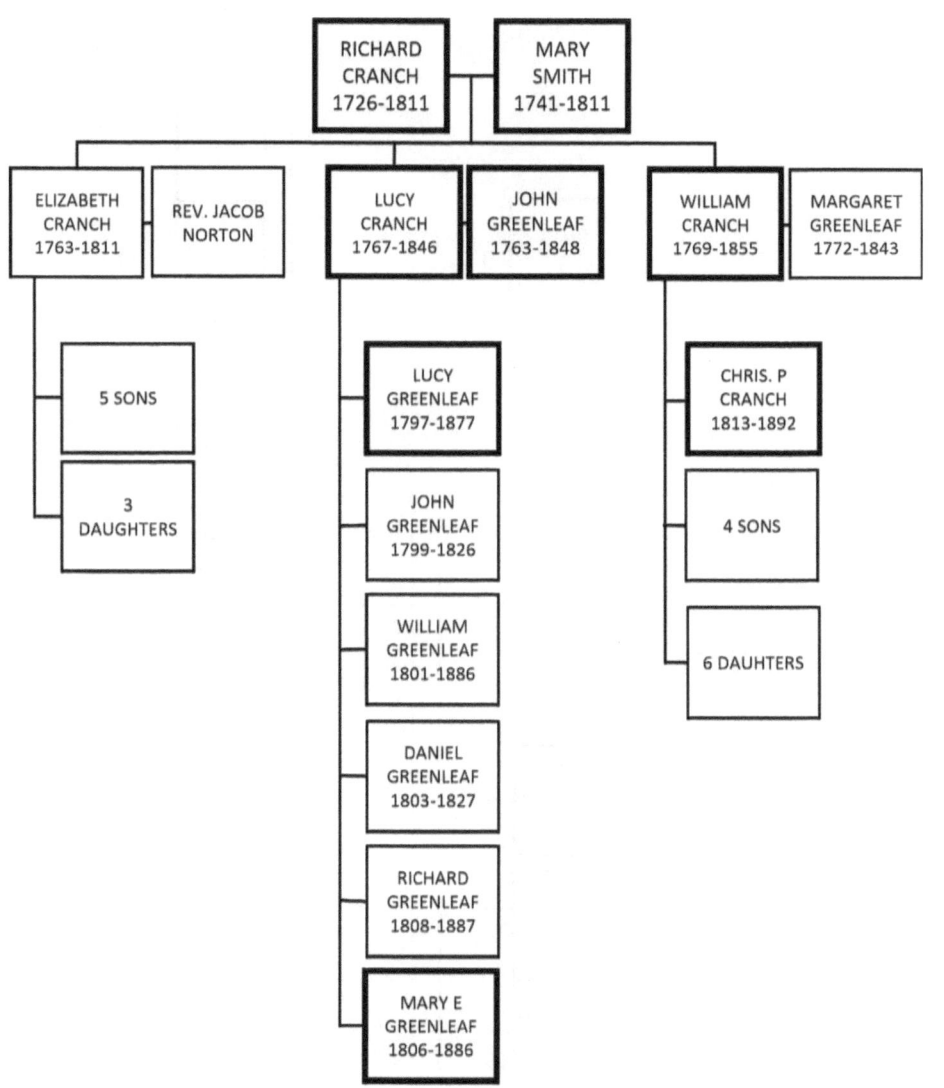

APPENDIX C
Dawes Brothers Marry Greenleaf Sisters

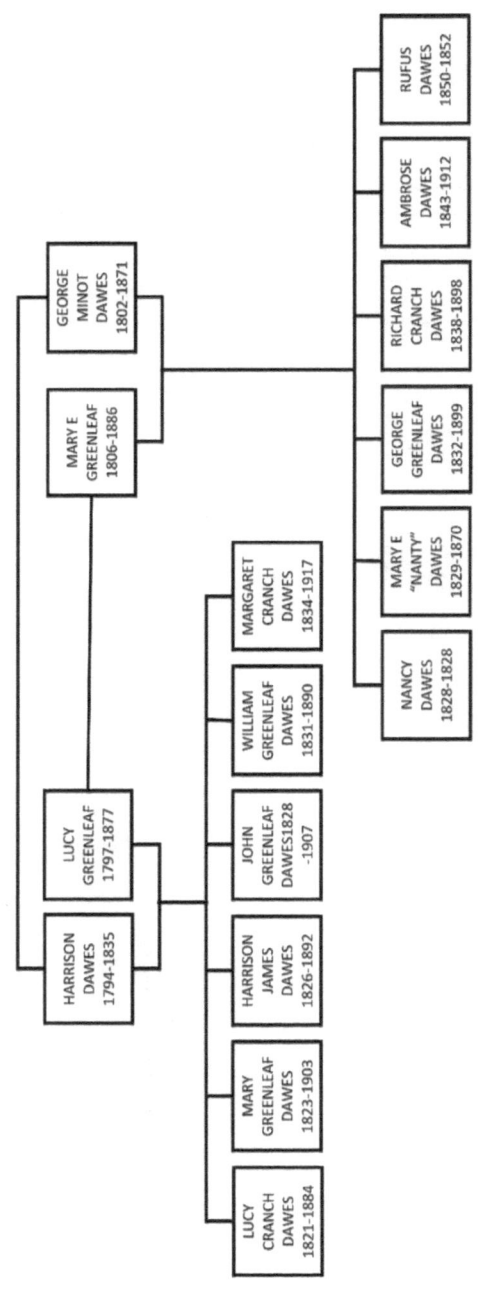

APPENDIX D
The Journey of George's Secretary

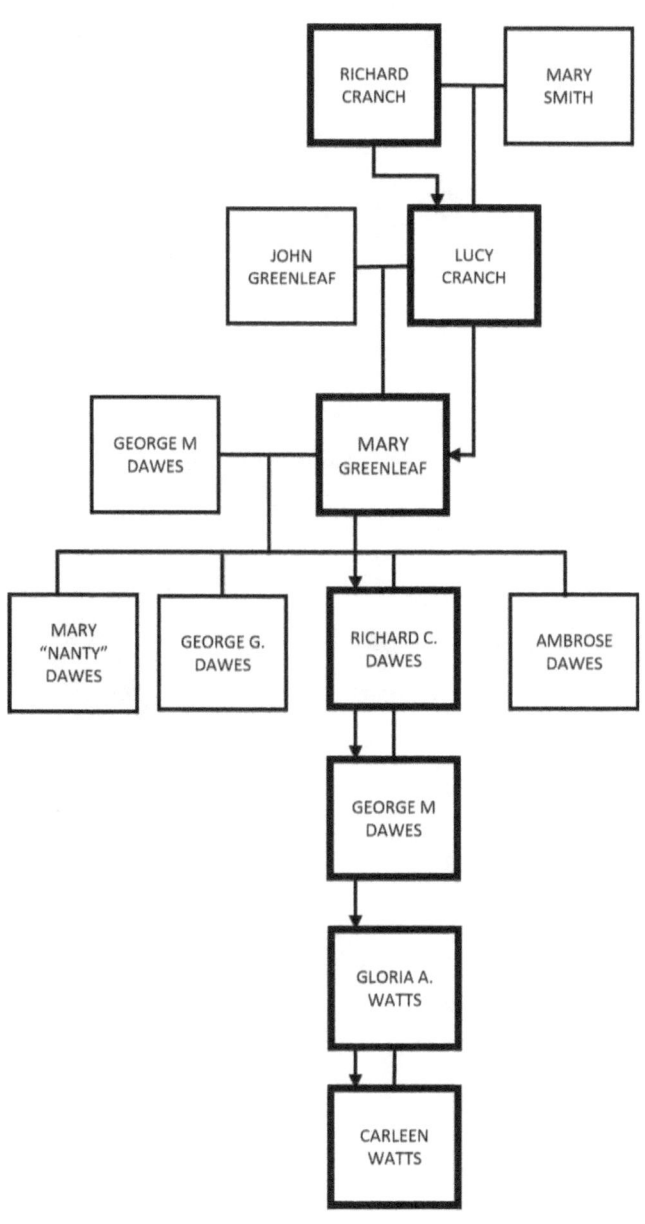

ACKNOWLEDGMENTS

Special Agents rarely get the opportunity to branch out into the world of creative writing, typically staying buried well within their restricted comfort zone, producing detailed and somewhat boring Reports of Investigation. I owe this attempt to bring the mystery of George's secretary into public view to Ondine LeBlanc, Editor at the Massachusetts Historical Society, who, after reviewing the collection of Nanty's letters and hearing my shortened tale as to how the letters came into my possession, simply said, "That's the story you should write about." Her words were few but they stirred something inside me. Thank you for this unimaginable challenge!

Making the transition from investigative report writing to creating a story someone would want to give up an evening to read could not have happened without the encouragement and extraordinary direction provided by Jenefer Angell (Passionfruit Projects). Unlike my high school English teachers, Jenefer's red edit track marks boosted my confidence and turned the self-publishing maze into a positive and rewarding experience. Who knew writing could be this much fun? You deserve a "Teacher of the Year" award! A book is nothing without an enticing cover. Wanna Johansson, the third member of this writing team, combined key individuals and evidence from my story to create this attention-grabbing cover. I am in awe of your creative talents.

As in any investigation, Special Agents often lack the specialized knowledge about the issue they are investigating. Techniques for developing the provenance of antique furniture were never discussed in my basic training academy. I must thank all of my expert witnesses: Robert Mussey, for sharing his research expertise and advising me on which issues to pursue but more importantly, his willingness to discuss and share his own findings about the life, family, and historic home of Richard and Mary Cranch; Brock Jobe for his "how to" instructional guide for finding possible identifiers belonging to an antique's owner, and for providing the most thorough inspection George's secretary had ever endured; and Erik Gronning for providing his unbiased evaluation of George's secretary early into my investigation, and then later for joining me inside one of those uncertain rabbit holes, never giving up on finding Margaret Dawes Ripley's personal notes about her great-great-grandmother's japanned high chest. To all of you, my case would not have been complete without your assistance and advice.

Of equal importance, I must also thank Josh Levine for taking me on the rollercoaster ride from hell during his auction and opening my eyes to the possible facts and connections each piece of the Dawes Collection might reveal about George's family.

A shout out to Jim Kennon who served as guinea pig for my first draft and offered his honest comments (both positive and negative) about my original storyline.

A special thank you to my dear departed friend, Renee Daphne Kimball, whose cherished gift gave me purpose during the COVID-19 pandemic lockdown. I think I can also speak on behalf of George's ancestors by saying thank you for rescuing Nanty's letters from an uncertain path and guarding them unselfishly until they could be re-united with the rest of the family's treasured collection.

Finally, thanks to my mother, Gloria Ann Watts (1927–2021). Readers, you have seen the terms "caregiver" and "caretaker" mentioned throughout this book. My mother met the definition of both, not by profession but by nature. From watching over her four younger siblings after her father's sudden death to befriending an elderly gentleman with the last name of Dawes, to nursing my father after a debilitating stroke, she fulfilled God's true purpose for her life. Few things brought my mother as much pleasure as being a caregiver—but one close contender was admiring newly discovered antiques. For her, being entrusted with the care of George's secretary was like winning the lottery.

Look for the Companion Book Coming Soon!

DISCOVERING NANTY DAWES

18th-Century Domestic Life through the Eyes of a Rare Young Artist

From
NANTY'S HOUSE

PUBLISHING

For some full-color images of George's secretary and more items from the Dawes Collection, visit WattsConsultingServices.com

sends his love to

do better than come back with

for Cuba; and the is stayin

the at their Uncle ton's

My Pine Knot has gone from off my

oing to preach, to preach at the

must this a cl

and ure U am

U R

nd in par r

ABOUT THE AUTHOR
Carleen A. Watts, CFE

Carleen served as a Special Agent (criminal investigator) for the United States government for over thirty-two years, working within the Inspectors General community investigating internal fraud for the US Departments of Agriculture, Defense, Veterans Affairs, and the Postal Service. During her tenure she also served as a Senior Instructor and Program Coordinator within the Financial Fraud Institute, a division of the Federal Law Enforcement Training Center in Glynco, Georgia. She continues to maintain the professional credential of Certified Fraud Examiner.

After retiring from federal service in 2006, she accepted a contract position with the Special Inspector General for Afghanistan Reconstruction (SIGAR), regaining her Special Agent title as she followed the path of US dollars sent to Afghanistan to support reconstruction projects. Her first year's assignment was spent in Kabul, Afghanistan, followed by five more years at the agency's headquarter office in Arlington, Virginia.

She graduated from California State University, Long Beach, with a BS degree in Criminal Justice/Law Enforcement and received additional basic and specialized law enforcement training from the Federal Law Enforcement Training Center.

Carleen lives in Phoenix, Arizona, where she enjoys being fully retired and spending time "investigating" her own family origins.

www.ingramcontent.com/pod-product-compliance
Lightning Source LLC
Chambersburg PA
CBHW030303130626
46549CB00002B/670